Trapped in a Partnership?

Emotional
Dependence

Uncover the Real Meaning Behind Your Fear of Being Alone
How to Navigate Your Way Out of Toxic Partnerships and
Towards True Self-Love

MARIA REED

Table of Contents

Introduction

Dear Reader,

Relationships and a sense of belonging and connection are, by their very nature, the most salient aspects of a fulfilling life and mental, physical, and spiritual health for most people. Humans are social beings. We need to be part of a group and have close relationships to thrive and feel at peace with ourselves and others. It is through our interactions with others that we discover ourselves, develop, and evolve. Healthy relationships are characterized by deep closeness and the ability to be open and vulnerable in order to be loved as we are.

Some individuals have a strong desire for connection and relationships. However, this can lead to a tendency to become emotionally dependent on their partners, where their sense of self and their needs become subordinate to the needs and desires of the other person. In healthy relationships, there is a balance of power and a shared creative approach to life and the relationship. Emotional dependency, on the other hand, creates a permanent imbalance where the emotionally dependent person feels powerless and at the mercy of the other person. Their attention and actions revolve around the other instead of being centered and active from within themselves.

In this book, you will learn about emotional dependency - what it is, how it develops, and how you can embark on a path towards freedom without having to let go of your desire for genuine connection. In fact, by cultivating a strong sense of self and inner awareness, those who are self-reliant can experience authentic openness, closeness, and intimacy. This ability can be learned and honed through a journey of healing and self-discovery. As we develop positive experiences with our own inner strength and self-worth, we come to realize that the most important relationship we will ever have is the one we have with ourselves.

In every relationship we enter, we bring ourselves along. Our experiences, fears, worries, doubts, but also our hopes, desires, talents, and unique qualities actively shape the relationship. The more we value and honor our own selves, the greater positive impact we can have on the relationship.

Emotional dependency arises when we become disconnected from ourselves and lose touch with our true selves. We can no longer accurately identify our own needs and prioritize ourselves. We start seeking external validation and fulfillment, believing that someone else is the key to feeling worthy, loved, and complete.

This book is intended for you if...

- ◆ You sense an emotional imbalance in your romantic relationship or other connections.
- ◆ You feel disconnected from yourself, and contact with your partner intensifies this feeling, leaving you with underlying sadness or uneasiness.
- ◆ You frequently feel helpless and powerless in the relationship, unable to meet your needs and desires.

- ◆ You feel that you are giving more than you are receiving.
- ◆ Your thoughts constantly revolve around your partner's needs and feelings.
- ◆ You feel responsible for regulating your partner's emotions.
- ◆ You feel the need to withdraw and make yourself scarce because your partner gives less than you, which makes you feel angry and helpless.
- ◆ You experience temporary fulfillment and joy in devotion to your partner, but this alternates with feelings of anger and disappointment.
- ◆ You wonder when it will be your turn to be taken care of.
- ◆ You ponder what true freedom in a relationship truly means.
- ◆ You desire to experience genuine closeness with another person in a healthy way without losing yourself.

Many individuals feel uncomfortable when they suspect they might be emotionally dependent. They may feel ashamed or deny the sense that something is amiss. They try to convince themselves to stay in the relationship and hold on. However, emotional dependence is nothing to be ashamed of. It is a common symptom and often a result of unmet childhood needs or boundary violations. The path to healing from emotional dependence lies in rediscovering your inherent dignity and vitality as a human being and cultivating a lifelong, affirming relationship with yourself without limitations.

Wishing you an enjoyable journey towards emotional freedom and self-empowerment!

Chapter 1

Am I Emotionally Dependent?

"A person can do without many things, but not without other people."

Ludwig Börne

Surely, you chose this book for a reason: You sense almost instinctively that something is wrong. At a certain point in your life, you feel an inner imbalance, an unpleasant development that perhaps worries you. You wonder what could be behind it. Perhaps you have a partner whom you love and admire, and with whom you enjoy being together. The relationship consumes you entirely, and at first glance, you want to say, "It's all right! I love this person with all my heart! I am such a lucky person to have found him/her."

But subconsciously, an uneasy gut feeling spreads. If this person is so important to you and you have chosen them, why don't you actually feel fulfilled, free, and happy?

You may find yourself thinking about the following possible signs:

- ◆ When you talk to others about the relationship, you feel an underlying need to defend it.

- When you talk about how happy you are, you feel a certain sadness accompanying it.
- The thought "something is sure to change soon" sounds familiar to you.
- You make special efforts to please the other person and long to receive the same in return.
- The relationship seems to strongly influence you - including your perception and evaluation, and you don't feel comfortable taking a different position.
- You feel inexplicably strange in your own life, and even worse or exceptionally comfortable when the other person is with you.
- It's hard for you to be alone.
- You perceive your own experiences and enjoyable moments as dull and lifeless when the other person is not with you or equally enthusiastic.
- You feel an inner ambivalence that temporarily resolves but keeps coming back - it strongly depends on the behavior of your partner. A part of you feels strongly attracted to the other, but a queasy feeling keeps you from experiencing pure joy and freedom in the relationship.
- You lack a sense of peace and stability.
- You fear losing the other person.
- You don't trust your own perception and tend to conform your behavior to please your partner.
- You often blame yourself when conflicts arise.
- You greatly admire the other person...
- ... and perhaps criticize them strongly because you feel powerless against them.
- You feel like you have to do everything you can to keep the relationship going...

- ... and make sure to be heard yourself. You fight for attention.
- You feel like the other person is moving slowly on their own path while you're rushing to keep up with them, following their path instead of your own.

Maybe you also pay strong attention to...

- Not burdening the other person.
- Not disturbing the other.
- Always looking beautiful/strong/confident, so as not to bore or annoy the other person.
- Avoiding conflicts.
- Adapting your plans to the other person.
- Behaving in a way that satisfies the other person, rather than yourself.
- Not stepping into the spotlight.
- Not stepping on the other person's toes.
- Doing too much or too little for the other person, depending on which way the imbalance leans.

Emotional dependence has many faces. It ranges from a slight imbalance in attending to mutual needs and desires to complete self-sacrifice and conformity on the part of the dependent person. One of the main characteristics of emotional dependence is the feeling of lack of freedom.

Inner freedom means:

- Being yourself without restrictions and the expectation of negative consequences.

- Being able to openly share the truth about your feelings, needs, and sensations without fear of being dismissed or rejected.
- Communicating your needs clearly and without feeling guilty while expecting your partner or the other person to respect and consider them.
- Devoting yourself to what is important to you, even if your partner or the other person is not enthusiastic about it.
- Feeling comfortable and confident in your own skin, regardless of the opinions of others.
- Recognizing your own importance and deserving respectful treatment from others, including loving connections on equal terms.

Do you tend to downplay, postpone, or hide needs that are truly important to you?

Do you rationalize your counterpart's behavior even when it hurts you?

Do you often feel the need to compromise in the relationship, with your own needs taking a backseat?

Do you find yourself engaging in self-sacrifice disguised as loving devotion?

Do you find it hard to imagine what it would feel like to have your heartfelt desires fulfilled in a friendship or partnership?

Do you subtly or overtly imply that your partner is only concerned with themselves?

Do you experience anger but then feel ashamed and apologize to avoid upsetting the other person?

Do you feel like a flag in the wind, constantly swayed by the influence of the other person?

Emotional dependence is always characterized by subliminal or overt fear: fear of loss, fear of making mistakes, fear of one's own courage, and fear of being alone. We often try to influence another person's behavior, hoping they will act in a way that benefits us or, at the very least, does not harm us.

Take a moment to circle the passages in this chapter that resonate with you. By doing so, you can gain insight into how emotional dependence may be manifesting in your relationship with a specific person or in your relationships in general.

The expression of emotional dependence is shaped by early childhood experiences. It is, therefore, valuable to examine the feelings and behaviors you identify in yourself or your counterpart. Ask yourself: Where does this feeling or perception come from? Does it remind me of a similar situation in the past? Are these patterns recurring with different people?

Additionally, circle the following phrases that you can relate to. You can replace the term "partner" with another person with whom you have an emotional dependence:

"When my partner appears distant and dismissive, I feel guilty."

"I often feel the need to prompt my partner to speak or take action."

"I have a tendency to want to please my partner even before they express any dissatisfaction."

"I struggle to imagine what it would be like if my partner were naturally affectionate and open with me."

"I often feel unheard by my partner, which leads me to question my self-worth and feel rejected."

Or:

"I have a partner who does a lot for me, but as soon as they're on their own, fear grips me - what if they find someone else they like better?"

"I believe that my partner loves me, but I struggle to behave freely and authentically."

"I tend to immediately change my behavior when my partner enters the room."

"I'm afraid of my partner discovering the real, vulnerable me and falling out of love because of it."

"I think about my partner from morning till night, and everything else interests me less and less."

"When I'm in a relationship, I often neglect my hobbies and friendships."

"I would rather chase after my partner and completely reshape my life for them than risk losing them."

"Can't I live without it if it bothers my partner? Making a small sacrifice for love is not a real sacrifice after all."

*

Now you may be wondering what emotional dependence actually means and where it starts. Isn't it healthy and normal for two people to embark on a new journey together that involves compromise once they enter into a relationship? Doesn't it require reevaluating and perhaps letting go of certain quirks and habits in order to do something good for each other? Doesn't love also mean that they miss each other when they're not around or that they want to share beautiful experiences with each other? When does love cross the line into dependence?

As a general rule, dependence arises when you can no longer freely be yourself without fearing negative consequences. Dependence is evident in self-sacrifice regarding aspects that define you and are important to you. It arises as a consequence of your boundaries being disrespected, abandoned, and ignored. On the other hand, love is saying yes to another person out of your own sense of wholeness, based on saying yes to yourself.

A healthy, loving relationship is built on the foundation of accepting and embracing everything within yourself, while also saying yes to another person who sees and appreciates all of you—or at least wants to see more and more. However, when a part of you says no to yourself in order to say yes to the other, you quickly find yourself in a state of dependency. As a natural consequence of self-denial, you now rely on the other person to fill this void within you. Unfortunately, emotionally dependent individuals often unconsciously seek out others who allow them to become emotionally dependent. In most cases, these individuals are not willing to replace your lack of self-acceptance with their affirmation of you—unless they unconsciously desire to be your savior. However, such a connection does more harm than good to both parties involved. It becomes increasingly challenging for you to sustain a healthy partnership or relationship focused on growth and healing if you must receive from your partner what you cannot first provide for yourself.

Emotional dependence serves as a substitute for saying yes to yourself—unconsciously, it is easier to fall into old patterns of saying yes to someone you admire rather than saying yes to yourself. Emotional dependency keeps you trapped in repetitive cycles. You avoid standing on your own and shaping your lives based on your genuine heartfelt feelings and needs. You yearn to be loved without fully showing up with everything that truly defines you. Thus, the need for validation, worthiness, and permission from another person emerges. Unfortunately, this need often leads to the opposite outcome: the partners of emotionally dependent individuals often respond with rejection, walls, and strong boundaries—some may even exploit the emotional dependency to their advantage.

By depending on others, you do not achieve what you truly need. Instead, you drift further away from your own inner core and lose the authentic ability to connect with others you genuinely resonate with.

Another common characteristic of emotionally dependent individuals is maintaining relationships with people who do not share their values and beliefs and often possess traits that are incompatible with the dependent person. Consequently, they become dependent on individuals and fall in love with personality types that normally wouldn't seem attractive for them. This also explains the feeling of moving away from oneself in the name of love, as they become more emotionally aligned with the other person's world than with their own.

Observation

Complete the following sentences in relation to the relationship in which you suspect emotional dependence:

I feel uncomfortable in relation to ...
I feel like I have to choose ... to avoid ...
I am afraid of ...
I wish my partner would give me ... as a gift. Instead, however, it is the order of the day ...
I don't feel free in the relationship...
I fall into fear and uncertainty when ...
In a relationship where I didn't feel dependent, here's what I would do differently: ...

Chapter 2

How Did I End Up Here?

"Unfulfilled wishes bind us far more than fulfilled ones."

Dami Charf, "Even Old Wounds Can Heal"

To explain how emotional dependence arises, it is necessary to take a journey into the past, to where it all began.

As a small baby, you were naturally completely and unrestrictedly dependent on your caregivers. Only physical functions such as digestion, breathing, and crying worked independently. To survive and feel safe, it was imperative that other people cared for you and prioritized your well-being over their own needs to a great extent. You had to be the center of everyone's attention so that you would be well emotionally, physically, and spiritually.

Take a moment to emotionally immerse yourself in the following thought: "I am the center of attention of someone I deeply love and adore. This person does everything to ensure that I am not only well, but truly well. I am fully fulfilled and happy."

Can you feel this state emotionally? What triggers you to imagine that someone else is doing everything for your well-being? What feelings and thoughts might automatically arise that could oppose this?

"I'm not worth that."

"I can't imagine that. I feel like I'm holding the other person back from things that are actually more important to them."

"I feel like a burden."

"I am hungry, physically or internally, but when I make this known, I disturb and draw anger rather than joyful devotion and love."

"I feel guilty about asking for too much."

These thoughts and feelings surface when you didn't receive the kind of attention you naturally deserve in your earliest childhood.

Many people find it difficult to feel and accept even this simple truth: "It is natural that I not only deserve loving attention but that I am fundamentally entitled to it. As a baby, I have a basic right to have my caregiver open up to me emotionally, physically, and emotionally. Only in this way can I grow up healthy and fulfilled. This state is ideal for my development and is basically designed that way by nature."

Many people have not experienced the basic emotional warmth and affection to the fullest extent in the first two years of life. For a variety of reasons, their parents were not able to mobilize all the energy to be fully there for their child.

In the animal kingdom, we can observe that it is the natural instinct of the mother to devote herself to raising the young without disturbance. If she is not able or willing to do so, the young must die. In humans, in addition to the instinct and biological readiness to nurture the child, the mental state and the conditions of the external circumstances also play an important role in the mother's/parents' ability to attend to their child. As a baby, we need not only physical closeness and nourishment to survive, but above all an open heart and warm, loving attention and care.

If you want, take a moment to reflect on this: As a baby, you sensed everything that was happening around you to an intense degree. You could instinctively sense the emotional states of your caregivers clearly and were forced to react to them in a certain way. If your mother took you in her arms but was tense while doing so, this tension passed directly onto you, triggering an alarm within your inner system. Why? Because your mother's tension directly affected your chances of physical, emotional, and spiritual survival. You were totally dependent on your parents not leaving you alone.

Every form of aloneness, rejection, or neglect leaves traces in our system. As a young child, we experience the world directly through contact with the people closest to us. Their limits, hurts, and inner struggles became a direct possible danger to our well-being.

Since no human being can flawlessly assume a parental role because they themselves are deeply shaped by their childhood experiences, hurts, fears, and unmet needs inevitably arise. These experiences shape certain beliefs about ourselves, our self-worth, our position in the world, in society, and in relationships.

If it has been suggested to us, even unintentionally, that we are a disturbance or a burden in our existence, this belief is deeply ingrained within us: "I am a disturbance. It would be better if I made myself invisible, small, if I were not there. I should take up as little space as possible."

Emotional dependence in childhood is thus natural and completely normal. However, as we grow older, it becomes a problem because these negative beliefs prevent us from meeting our counterparts without these fears. We continue to carry around the same unmet needs and project them onto potential friendships, love relationships, and even superficial connections.

Most of these longings and needs remain hidden in the subconscious for a long time. Then you may wonder why you keep attracting similar partners with whom you have the same experiences, interestingly enough, always evoking your old pain.

Your beliefs about yourself and your self-worth are constantly active, and as long as they are not resolved and changed, you automatically behave in a certain way that unconsciously sends the message to others: "I am not worthy of your attention. I disrupt your everyday life and have too many demands. I don't think you can truly love me with all your heart..." and so on.

Exercise: Beliefs

When you feel emotionally ready, take a moment to reflect on your past:

How much do you know or suspect about the atmosphere that surrounded you and the way you were treated within your family during that time? To what extent were your parents and close caregivers able to respond to you? Did you experience encouragement and closeness? Were they wholeheartedly happy that you were there? Did you feel warmth and security?

During this exercise, it is helpful to emotionally detach yourself from your experiences and objectively write down what it must have been like during that time. Examine your environment at that time, considering its physical condition as well as the emotional and spiritual aspects, such as a growth-oriented and loving support system. The spiritual development and a child-oriented, nurturing environment are just as important as the ability of your parents to approach you with love and acceptance.

Once you have completed this examination of the past, turn your attention to the present:
How do you currently organize your everyday life and relationships? What is the atmosphere like in your relationships? Do you feel like you are in the right place? Do you feel cared for, loved, safe, and secure? Are you engaging in activities that bring you joy? Do you allow yourself to give to others without feeling guilty? Or do you notice emotional coldness, fear of being too much, a constant unsatisfied longing in your relationships?
Based on this analysis, take some time to write down your inner beliefs about yourself and your self-worth.

Ideally, as a child, your needs were fulfilled, and you were able to gradually become independent in a curious, open, and expectant manner, motivated by a safe and loving environment. This would be the ideal circumstance. However, you have probably developed a list of beliefs that indicate that your childhood did not provide the best starting conditions.

But don't despair. Imperfection, gaps, and flaws are part of life. The moment you realize that things don't have to remain as they were then, your journey as an independent person, working towards stability, begins. Today, as an adult, you are no longer dependent on the decisions made by those who cared for you in the past.

In the process of healing and self-realization, it is now about reclaiming your natural self-worth, piece by piece. Remember, it was your birthright to be unconditionally dependent, to receive love and protection without having to do anything for it. The fact that you didn't fully experience this doesn't change your inherent birthright.

As an adult, you now have the opportunity to meet your own needs and desires in a way that is truly beneficial for you. You can explore and identify the beliefs that hold you back from recognizing your self-worth and shaping your life accordingly. Additionally, as adults, another birthright is activated: the right to free choice.

In our social and societal structures, there are prevailing systems worldwide that do not align with this right. Inhumane circumstances, such as religious constraints, hierarchical structures, abuse of power, and violence, undermine the natural right to free choice for every individual.

However, these circumstances cannot override the inherent right in any way, just as your childhood experiences cannot change your natural right to receive loving care in a state of complete dependence.

To bring about a deep transformation in your life and experience, it is helpful to constantly remind yourself that the natural and original rights of every human being and all life still exist. By rediscovering and embracing your right to free choice based on your natural self-worth, you can gradually change your negative beliefs.

How Beliefs Shape Your Reality

It is relatively easy to identify your negative beliefs within your current living environment. But how is this possible?

Everything you allow and permit in your life is based on the fundamental alignment of your subconscious mind. If you find yourself in an emotionally dependent relationship today, a closer examination will reveal the corresponding negative beliefs about your self-worth and abilities.

For years, Jasmin has repeatedly dealt with partners who become annoyed by her neediness, respond with indignation, show brusqueness and dismissiveness, and eventually leave her in frustration.

Peter, on the other hand, falls deeply in love with beautiful women who confidently reject him and make it clear that he is not worthy of them.

Mary constantly faces betrayal, which inflicts deep emotional pain and makes her question her own worth.

David goes to great lengths for his girlfriend, sacrificing his hobbies, cutting off contact with friends, and giving her constant attention in an effort to keep her. Ironically, his efforts result in the opposite outcome: his partner starts to dominate him, complains about his lack of assertiveness, and becomes angrier the more he tries.

Irena repeatedly finds herself in situations where she only receives atten-tion when she completely sets herself aside and allows the other person to unload their own issues. She is highly regarded as a listener, but no one ever asks how she is doing.

Nicole, despite being in a long-term relationship, suffers from emotional coldness. She doesn't dare interrupt her partner, express her needs, or even take up space to be heard with undivided attention. As a result, she feels herself sinking deeper into loneliness. Unconsciously, she hopes to gain more attention by being accommodating, but instead, she experiences even more coldness or harsh rejection. Nicole holds onto hope for improvement, enduring this for ten long years.

What all these individuals have in common is that they repeat-edly encounter experiences that align with their beliefs. Some-one who truly believes they are lovable would never endure a decade of emotional unavailability from a partner.

Note: There is a significant distinction between knowing that you are lovable and actually feeling it. Knowledge based solely on reason does not lead to change because it is not deeply anchored within us. True change stems from aligning with our current, actual beliefs, which are shaped by our experiences. It is only on this level that we can create new experiences and make conscious decisions that feel right and good.

Your behaviors feel coherent when they align with your inner beliefs. The real challenge lies in the fact that even negative and harmful experiences can feel coherent at a profound level be-cause they correspond to your ingrained beliefs. It is important to remember that coherence does not equate to being right or good. Just because something feels coherent out of habit does not mean it should remain that way or that it is the right path for you. Your experiences are not based on what is objectively right, but rather on what you secretly believe to be right.

Exercise: World of Experience

On a large sheet of paper, create a map representing your experiences. Start by drawing a shape that symbolizes a country - the country of your life up until now. Next to this country, create a legend using different colors.

Example:
Yellow - represents the belief of not deserving attention.
Red - represents the belief of always being last in line.
Orange - represents the belief of being disruptive.

Include colors for positive beliefs as well:
Blue - represents the belief in success.
Green - represents the belief in beauty.

... and so on.

Now, use the corresponding colors to paint your life country, assigning each belief to appropriate parts of the country. Take note of how much space each belief occupies and to what extent they influence your overall well-being.

This exercise will provide you with a better understanding of the current state of your life. The colors will visually demonstrate how much your beliefs impact your experiences. Colors may overlap, so feel free to adapt the exercise according to your own perception.

If you'd like, you can also create another map with new beliefs, reflecting your desired outlook for change. Add colors to represent aspects of life you wish to have, such as
attention or tenderness, assigning them a significant portion of the new map.

Observe how the actual conditions differ from your desired landscape and take note of any gaps that need to be
addressed.

Subconscious and Attachment Behavior

The *"subconscious"* is the hidden realm that essentially governs
our emotions, thoughts, and behaviors. Over eighty percent of
our personality resides there, while only a small portion emerges as conscious awareness, akin to the tip of an iceberg visible
above water. The subconscious, like the submerged part of the
iceberg, exerts far greater control over our decisions, percep-
tions, and personality than we consciously realize.

Our subconscious mind is shaped by our earliest experiences
as infants and even during the prenatal stage. How our environment responded to us, our mother's thoughts, feelings, and
self-perception, the process of birth, and whether we perceived
the world as safe or not - all of these factors decisively shape
our emotional disposition and approach to the world up to
the present day. The subconscious mind interprets our current
experiences based on our past experiences, making it challenging to bring about lasting and rapid changes. It often requires
delving into the subconscious through various methods and

healing approaches to understand how we were shaped and to effect mindful and profound changes in the present.

In the context of emotional dependence, our subconscious mind plays a crucial role. It holds the key to why it is difficult for us to feel secure on our own and why we often find ourselves dependent on individuals who harm us repeatedly.

Underlying this dynamic is the concept of attachment behavior, which is also developed during early childhood. Our relationship with primary attachment figures molds our understanding of attachment, our perception of what is normal, and our beliefs about ourselves.

If our attachment experiences were secure, we had a stable anchor through our relationship with our caregiver, enabling us to develop a sense of security and a positive self-image. We felt loved, valued, and important, experiencing open and affectionate attention. With a reliable and emotionally available caregiver, we could confidently form attachments, trusting that they would not abandon us.

However, insecurity, ambivalence, and dysfunctional attachments to our caregivers imprint different beliefs in our subconscious. Those who did not experience secure attachment in early childhood carry this information within their subconscious. Based on this information, our subconscious also influences our partner selection and significantly shapes the course of communication and connection within relationships.

This is how emotional dependence develops in adulthood. Dependency arises when a person hopes for something from another person who does not provide it, yet sees no way to break free from the connection without risking harm.

Especially in cases of insecure-ambivalent or dysregulated attachment behavior from a child's caregiver, emotional dependence can persist into adulthood. When a caregiver struggles to regulate themselves, unable to adequately meet their own emotional needs, they are often unavailable to the child at times when the child seeks attachment. By rejecting, being absent, aggressive, or otherwise unavailable, the caregiver triggers stress in the child, who, paradoxically, desires even more closeness to find security. The child finds themselves in a bind, wanting to bond with the person whose behavior triggers inner turmoil.

Dami Charf addresses this phenomenon in her book "Even Old Wounds Can Heal," stating, *"Paradoxically, rejections further reinforce attachment-seeking behavior. The more rejecting the parents are, the more children seek their presence. Often, this manifests as inappropriate loyalty to rejecting or even abusive parents. Additionally, these individuals continue to seek their parents' affirmation and love well into adulthood, sometimes even in old age. Unfulfilled desires bind us far more than fulfilled ones."*

This passage highlights the dilemma of emotional dependence. The more we feel rejected and dismissed, the more we hope for a change in the behavior of our loved one - the person we desire to provide us with security, belonging, and protection. The issue is not the need for attachment itself, as it is a fundamental human need necessary for survival and well-being. The problem lies from how our subconscious is influenced by past experiences. Many people have not experienced a secure and healthy attachment, and they suffer the consequences of unhealthy attachments to their caregivers during that time. Every unresolved and unintegrated experience from that period repeats itself in current relationships through similar patterns. While we may present as desired and loved partners to a small extent (the visible tip of the iceberg), the greater part of us, over eighty percent, is still the child carrying unfulfilled attachment needs from the past into the partnership.

This subconscious program operates in the background between partners, influencing the interpretation of all interpersonal events. We tend to take our partner's behavior personally and relate it to ourselves. Emotional dependence arises when we become emotionally attached to our partner and not only fulfill their desire for connection, but also encounter their unresolved issues and limitations. If we haven't learned to establish the necessary self-reliance and security within ourselves, we project these needs onto our partner, and our subconscious takes over, perpetuating the cycle of emotional dependence.

Exercise: Explore the Subconscious

Begin by writing down the names of the close attachment figures you had in your earliest childhood. Reflect on the type of bond they provided. Were they able to offer closeness, affection, and love? Were they open, affectionate, and loving? Also, try to recall any difficulties they had or any challenges you remember from that time.

If you have limited memories, pay attention to your body and feelings. How does it feel for you to emotionally open up to someone close to you? Do you feel safe and secure?

Does it feel familiar to be curious and open in the world while also feeling protected? Take note of any contact or connection that you find challenging. Are you able to establish healthy boundaries easily?

Now, examine your attachment behaviors in the following areas:

- Physical contact
- Expression of affection
- Feelings of safety and security
- Ability to communicate one's needs
- Potential feelings of guilt when the focus is on oneself
- Potential fear of upsetting the other person
- Ambivalent needs for both closeness and freedom

Based on how your attachment behaviors are shaped, you can often deduce the kind of attachment experiences you had in your earliest childhood. Your subconscious mind draws upon these experiences to shape your present relationships. Furthermore, write down the automatic thoughts that come to your mind when your partner fails to meet your need for commitment in a loving and open manner. For example:

- No one is there for me - I am alone.
- I am superfluous.
- It would be better if I were gone.
- Nobody enjoys doing anything with me - I'm boring.
- I don't want to be there anymore because no one loves me.

Important Note: If you find this process overwhelming, do not hesitate to seek professional help. Memories from our past can be highly emotionally charged, and we do not have to face the integration and healing journey alone. Feeling safe and supported along the way is crucial for our well-being and growth.

Dependent on Mom and Dad: The Other as a Parental Authority

As a result of the natural and necessary dependency between children and their caregivers, they often find themselves in nearly unsolvable internal stalemate situations. The child yearns for love and affection, but not from just anyone—it seeks these from its specific caregiver, the one it has attached to for security and protection. It desires someone who will take responsibility for its well-being, and that person is none other than the caregiver, not a stranger or someone else. The child longs for a sense of mutual belonging and encouragement, to be welcomed by the person it has formed a bond with.

Does this need sound familiar to your partner or other close individuals? You'll understandably feel that it doesn't make sense when a stranger shows you the affection you truly desire from your partner. While you may feel flattered, your heart will only truly be touched and warmed if the tenderness comes from the person you have formed an attachment with.

If, for various reasons, parental caregivers were unable to fulfill these needs for their child, the child found itself in a position of responsibility it should never have been burdened with. It had to manage the consequences of unmet natural needs, which can be an inadequate and negatively impactful task. On one hand, the child can never fully assume this responsibility, and on the other hand, it has to deviate from the natural order.

The adaptation to external circumstances leads to a detachment from oneself and one's own needs, resulting in the belief that one will never receive what is truly needed. The child feels compelled to conform in order to avoid getting lost. In order to escape the immense and unbearable pain, a part of the self is split off. Ultimately, resignation sets in, and the survival and functional mode is activated.

In adulthood, a person carries this behavior into relationships. It becomes challenging for them to truly feel themselves, to stand independently, and to avoid succumbing to the fear of abandonment when expressing opposing viewpoints. The partner becomes the embodiment of the parental authority from the past, which the person has never fully let go of. They have failed to break free from dependence and find security within themselves. This is also a consequence of the inability to acknowledge and have their own needs met. Once again, the person abandons themselves and adapts to the social environment in order to survive and secure even a minimum of attention—just as they did in the past.

In a partnership, this often results in the partner assuming the role of the one who repeatedly fails to meet needs and desires, leaving the emotionally dependent person to fend for themselves.

Chapter 3

How Does Emotional Dependence Manifest Itself?

"Each creature is connected to another,
and every being is bound by another."

Hildegard of Bingen

Emotional dependence can manifest itself in various ways. It is not limited to individuals who excessively rely on their partner and constantly seek their validation. Even those who appear independent on the surface can still experience emotional dependence. At its core, emotional dependence refers to the inability to self-regulate and meet one's own needs in a healthy manner. In this chapter, we will explore different symptoms that indicate the presence of emotional dependence. These symptoms can range from subtle imbalances to more pronounced dependencies, often accompanied by other psychological and physical manifestations that highlight an underlying imbalance within one's own soul.

Clinging

Clinging is indicative of an anxious attachment style. Whenever the partner asserts their independence by expressing their own opinions, distancing themselves internally or externally, or otherwise asserting their individuality, the emotionally dependent person's alarm bells start ringing. Old attachment patterns resurface, and the dependent individual feels an urgent need to beg, plead, and cling to the other person for attention. Instead of finding stability within themselves and trusting in the relationship, they resort to trying to control the other person through clinging behavior. The need for control manifests as a display of weakness, aiming to draw attention to oneself. Those who cling often sacrifice their own hobbies and interests, focusing their attention solely on their partner and rarely letting them out of their sight. They strive to become indispensable, seeking shared activities, establishing mutual circles of friends, and familiarizing themselves with all of their partner's acquaintances. In the event of a conflict, the clinging person tries to seek forgiveness if they have gone too far, feeling ashamed of their outbursts or differing viewpoints. The other person becomes the authority figure expressing disapproval through raised eyebrows or disapproving looks. This triggers immense pain in the clinging person, intensifying their need to repair the relationship. However, their notion of "making things right" often involves appeasement rather than engaging in equal and collaborative communication to seek resolution. The clinging person may not even be aware of the possibility of a relationship based on equality, as they have not experienced it before. Restoring the connection means reestablishing the old order of fitting in, adapting, and avoiding abandonment, even if this dynamic is ultimately detrimental to their well-being in the long run.

Clinging behavior includes the following actions:

- ◆ Clamoring, ranting, and crying
- ◆ Exerting control through text messages, contacts, and calls
- ◆ Suspiciously seeking information
- ◆ Making excessive phone calls
- ◆ Apologizing excessively and frequently
- ◆ Trying to become indispensable to the other person
- ◆ Going above and beyond to fulfill the other person's needs

→ Any behavior intended to manipulate the other person into staying with the clinging individual.

Stonewalling

Stonewalling, which refers to emotional inaccessibility and stubbornness towards one's partner, is another indication of emotional dependence. It manifests as a defensive attitude towards the partner's feelings and needs, a refusal to engage in empathetic and equal communication, and a tendency to terminate conversations when they become emotionally charged. It also involves an unwillingness to change one's own behavior or to provide the other person with the space and support they require.

How can walls be a sign of emotional dependence? At first glance, it may appear to demonstrate a sense of independence. However, partners of emotionally dependent individuals often describe them as emotionally cold, disinterested, and unreachable.

Let's recall the childhood experiences when the dependent child did not receive the love and attention they needed. Many individuals who engage in stonewalling today had been in the unpleasant situation of seeking attention and being coldly rejected. Consequently, they learned to suppress their own neediness because it evoked feelings of guilt, shame, and being perceived as too demanding or disruptive.

When individuals who stonewall encounter a needy partner in their current relationships, it triggers these unpleasant emotions from their past, which they can hardly tolerate. In response, they become emotionally distant, refusing to acknowledge the other person's neediness, and sometimes even reacting with anger or disgust towards their partner's vulnerability.

Another factor contributing to stonewalling behavior lies in the experiences with parents who exhibited various forms of abuse towards the child. When parents unconsciously place blame on their child for their emotional instability and expect the child to fulfill their emotional needs, the child may eventually become emotionally rigid, hardened, and resistant to the emotional needs of others. In this process, the child denies and disconnects from their own emotional needs, as they are disregarded and pushed to the margins due to the self-centeredness of the parents. The child primarily serves as an object for the parents' projections.

Later, in partnerships, stonewalling becomes evident as a lack of connection with one's own emotional needs. Nevertheless, the stonewalling partner is emotionally dependent—specifically in terms of attempting to communicate their needs through stonewalling: "I need something right now, but I cannot express it." This emotional dependency arises from the inability to communicate with the other person in a healthy and effective manner.

Emotional walls are often accompanied by a strong perception of being trapped within an inner prison or enveloped by a shadow that weighs on the soul. Individuals who engage in stonewalling often wish that their partner could instinctively understand their needs and choose to pay attention to them. The feeling of an inner prison reflects a longing to connect with one's own needs and desires. The emotional dependence is evident in the fact that the stonewaller requires a counterpart against whom they can erect walls. They need someone to defend themselves against to avoid feeling completely detached and isolated.

Many individuals who tend to build emotional walls report that it is only through this form of self-protection that they can assert their boundaries and feel a sense of self. In the absence of someone to guard against, these individuals often experience profound loneliness. They struggle to embrace genuine closeness, yet when they are all alone, they are primarily afraid of themselves.

Expect Validation from the Partner

Additionally, many emotionally dependent individuals have a tendency to seek constant confirmation from their partners for everything they do. Their inner child is constantly seeking validation, sending the message, "Tell me I'm doing this right!" They consistently ask the other person, whether directly or indirectly, questions like, "How should I handle this situation? What are your thoughts on this? Will you still like me if I make this decision?"

Young children naturally exhibit this behavior as they rely on reassurance and feedback from their caregivers to navigate the world and establish a sense of security. Everything they do is a new experience, and they seek the caregiver's validation that their actions are safe and accepted. Through this instinctual process of seeking feedback, young children develop a comprehensive understanding of what is appropriate and desired and how they can explore the world in their own way.

However, if this feedback is absent and the child is left to their own devices, they may lack the necessary support to develop a sense of security and belonging. Their curiosity and judgment may not develop in a healthy manner, and they become prone to insecurity and negative emotions.

Those who require constant validation from their partner to feel secure in the relationship often experienced love and support as a child only when their behavior aligned with what the caregiver deemed appropriate. The caregiver may have paid little attention to the child, or attention was mainly negative. Believing that relationships are based on conditions and that love is withheld based on one's performance may have been prevalent during that time. Emotionally dependent individuals are convinced that they must conform to others' expectations and seek validation from their partner. This behavior can even extend to choosing clothes based on whether the partner approves of the style. They may alter their opinions to align with their partner's, feeling significant distress when they hold a different view or have no independent opinion at all. They mold themselves in a way that externally mirrors and aligns with their partner's life and inner world through their behavior. Internally, they repeatedly turn to their partner, attentively listening for any signs of detachment, loss of interest, anger, or disturbance.

This symptom is often particularly noticeable when it comes to decision-making. These individuals struggle to act based solely on their own feelings and take responsibility for their choices without being reliant on others' opinions. Emotional dependence manifests not only in the context of the partnership but also in relation to social groups or other individuals with whom they seek friendship. They constantly ask themselves questions like: "Would this person approve of my decision and like me more as a result?" or "Would this person turn towards me or away from me based on my choice?" Their own feelings follow this back-and-forth dynamic as they imagine how others would feel and subsequently experience the same emotions themselves. Thus, the external standards of others become the guiding force in their own lives, rather than being grounded in their own sense of self. This difficulty is particularly evident in individuals who had limited freedom and opportunities to shape their own lives during childhood. Strict parents, for instance, rarely asked questions like "How do you feel about it?" or "What do you want?" Instead, they issued orders and expected the child to unquestioningly comply with their decisions.

Control Issues

The need to control one's partner stems from the fear that the person will engage in actions, internal processes, or thoughts that are unfamiliar to the emotionally dependent individual. This fear can be unsettling and trigger a sense of losing control over one's own life.

Individuals with control issues often attempt to influence their partner's motives, decisions, behaviors, and have a strong desire to be constantly informed and involved. They fear that the consequences of their partner's actions may affect them in ways they cannot bear.

This behavior can be rooted in a childhood where parents consistently made decisions without considering the child's input, leading the child to internalize feelings of insignificance and powerlessness. No matter how hard the child tried to gain attention or assert their opinions and needs, their attempts seemed futile.

As adults, individuals with control issues may feel dependent on their partner's decisions, perceiving limited options: either go along with what the partner wants or face undesirable consequences. The underlying feeling of helplessness and powerlessness persists, particularly when the partner engages in actions or experiences internal processes that the affected individual struggles to understand or evaluate.

Emotional dependency is evident in the lack of confidence in one's own ability to assert oneself and exercise personal power. Expressing dissenting views or asserting personal boundaries can lead to painful reactions that dismiss the individual's concerns with statements like, "I don't care about your needs. Either comply or don't."

Under these circumstances, it becomes challenging to maintain a relationship on equal footing. The affected individual is constantly on edge, chronically stressed, and views the world, including the relationship, as a place where they must always be prepared for unwanted developments and the associated pain. Relaxation seems unattainable.

Some individuals even report having distressing dreams where they find themselves in terrible situations, yet they feel immobilized and powerless to leave or express their disagreement. These dreams are accompanied by a profound sense of helplessness and immobility.

Manipulation

Manipulation occurs when we feel compelled to engage in behaviors intended to persuade others to act or think in a specific way. It often starts innocently but can have disastrous consequences. For instance, when a parent threatens to withhold sweets from their child unless they immediately brush their teeth, they are resorting to manipulation. In relationships, emotionally dependent individuals often employ manipulative tactics to exert control or elicit the affection, tenderness, and attention they desire.

They have not learned to clearly express their needs and allow the other person to decide whether or not to fulfill them, or to draw appropriate boundaries and consequences. However, this does not lead to emotionally dependent individuals obtaining what they truly long for. Subconsciously, they recognize that anything gained through manipulation lacks authenticity. It does not arise from free will and is therefore essentially worthless. The aim is not to obtain affection by any means necessary but to receive love willingly and as a genuine gift. Only then can it truly nourish us, benefit us, and have a healing effect.

Manipulation shields us from the pain of rejection, but it simultaneously blocks the path to fulfilling love and genuine closeness. In this sense, it prevents the other person from showing their true self and only allows them to deliver what the manipulator desires.

Manipulative dynamics can be challenging to recognize. Many people believe that only highly narcissistic individuals engage in manipulative behaviors and take advantage of others. However, even emotionally dependent individuals who are deeply sensitive, empathetic, and loving can be highly manipulative. Their fear of rejection and the withdrawal of love drives them to do whatever it takes to keep the other person satisfied, avoid conflict, and maintain a sense of order. Yet, this behavior is detrimental to achieving equal footing and fostering genuine connections within the relationship.

Those who resort to manipulation learned in their childhood that their needs, perspectives, and desires were not important and that they did not receive attention solely because they were loved. They had to devise strategies to secure attention, make their needs known, and ensure they were noticed.

Typical manipulative behaviors include:

- Adopting a particularly kind and gentle tone of voice, aiming to regulate the other person's emotions rather than setting healthy boundaries.
- Calculating how to phrase something to persuade the other person to change their stance.
- Concealing one's true feelings, appearing vulnerable, and inducing guilt in others.
- Making the other person feel like they have failed.
- Provoking jealousy in the other person.
- Engaging in dramatic displays or actions.
- Seeking revenge as a means to assert control or wake the other person up to their actions.

Self-sacrifice

Self-sacrifice is one of the most profound stages of emotional dependence. When an individual has lost themselves and willingly relinquished their sense of self in the relationship, they have forsaken their values, resigned themselves, and surrendered to their fate. They are unable to assert themselves, stand up for their needs, actively participate in shaping the relationship, or engage with their partner on an equal footing. These individuals often sacrifice everything they hold dear in order to avoid losing the other person. For instance, many fathers may abandon their children after a separation to please a new, jealous spouse. Women may distance themselves from their friends, withdraw from their social circles, and remain at home with an aggressive, self-dependent, or even violent husband.

While these examples highlight specific genders, it is important to note that self-sacrifice can occur in any relationship and is not limited to a particular gender.

Other forms of self-sacrifice manifest as resigned, addictive behaviors. Many people turn to substances such as alcohol or cigarettes or engage in other harmful behaviors to redirect their anger, shame, and guilt toward their own bodies. They have lost respect for themselves and find it difficult to look themselves in the mirror. The partner upon whom they have become dependent may exhibit aggression, contemplate separation, or try to distance themselves from them. In some cases, both partners remain in a long-lasting relationship where the dependent partner's addiction benefits the other. However, both parties generally suffer from profoundly low self-esteem, and their childhood wounds resurface in their adult relationship.

Self-sacrifice does not occur when everything has already fallen apart. It begins with a "yes" when a "no" would have been appropriate but was never uttered due to fear of rejection and anger. It starts when compromise is no longer a mutual decision made on equal terms but rather when the individual feels compelled to abandon their own inner truth to maintain the relationship. When one's integrity and authenticity can no longer be upheld to save the relationship, the path to self-sacrifice has already been embarked upon.

Self-sacrifice represents the survival and coping mechanism that children adopt when they can only survive in their environment by denying their true selves. They must gloss over their circumstances, disregard their own desires, and betray themselves to fit in. Loyalty to their surroundings becomes paramount as they forsake themselves to avoid the crushing loneliness and the feeling of being an outcast.

Other Symptoms of Emotional Dependence

Emotional dependence emerges when we no longer feel connected to ourselves and our bodies, struggle to directly access our sensations and needs, and find it challenging to establish healthy boundaries and connections with others. This lack of attachment stems from an inability to self-regulate, as explained by Dami Charf in her book "Even Old Wounds Can Heal." When we cannot self-regulate, meaning we struggle to calm ourselves and reconnect with our inner selves, we often seek external support, which frequently manifests as emotional dependence on others.

Many people associate emotional dependence primarily with the belief that they cannot live without someone, fear of loss, and a tendency towards self-sacrifice in romantic relationships. However, there are other patterns and behaviors that also indicate emotional dependence.

Emotional dependence may manifest as:

- Difficulty in regaining composure and calming oneself without relying on another person.
- Lack of inner security regarding one's self-worth.
- Constantly seeking validation from others to prove one's worth.

- Abandoning one's own values to avoid being abandoned by others.
- Adapting to new circumstances in a way that conceals one's true essence.
- Inability to relax and establish connections in the presence of others.
- Needing others' opinions due to a fear of distrusting one's own intuition.
- Struggling to independently shape one's own life without assuming loneliness in the process.

Inspiration

Take a moment to write a letter to yourself, filled with understanding and loving words regarding the signs that may indicate emotional dependence within you. As you engage in this exercise, remember to avoid using terms like "incapacity" or "emotional dependency." While these words serve the purpose of conveying understanding and insights on an intellectual level, it is important to connect with your soul on an emotional level by using appropriate and personal language. Through this approach, you can effectively address your feelings and strengthen the connection with yourself.

By gaining a deeper understanding of yourself and these patterns, you lay the foundation for inner growth and transformation. This understanding is essential for developing an inner willingness to gradually let go of old habits, allowing for healing, integration, and meaningful change to occur.

Chapter 4
Finding A Way Forward

"Our actions should be guided by the ever-living awareness that humans are not free in their thoughts, emotions, and actions, but rather bound by causality, much like the celestial bodies in their movements."

Albert Einstein

Emotional dependency is a deeply ingrained pattern that permeates our emotional being, our body's memory, our neural pathways, and consequently, our thoughts and behaviors. It arises as a response to the threat of being left alone, rejected, and abandoned - an instinctual fear of destruction. Our task is to find a way to confront this fear in a healthy manner, allowing the structures of dependence to be replaced by genuine connections with ourselves and others. Through this inner work, we open ourselves to the possibility of experiencing the sense of connectedness that we yearn for.

What Past Relationship Underlies the Dependency?

The manifestation of emotional dependency always refers to past relationships, typically those with our primary attachment figures. In our present interactions, we unconsciously reenact the dynamics of those earlier relationships, seeking to heal the old wounds and fill the gaps that were left unfilled.

To gain clarity in this process, we need a discerning perspective that arises from mindful self-reflection. Take a moment to examine the relationship in which you suspect emotional dependency. Observe your behaviors, fears, worries, beliefs, and emotional patterns. Do any of these patterns feel familiar to you? Can you trace them back to your experiences with your mother, father, or other significant caregivers?

Also, observe your current partner or companion. Do you notice any similarities to past significant others? Initially, you may be inclined to dismiss such observations, especially if you consciously chose a partner who seems completely different from your parents. Perhaps you sought new experiences by selecting a calm and peaceful partner, hoping to avoid the fear of explosive outbursts and to feel safe. However, over time, you might notice subtle aspects in your partner's character that still resonate with your past experiences. While the behaviors may differ, you sense a similar lack of presence, passivity, being overlooked, broken promises, or self-centeredness. The outer expression may vary, but the underlying emotions remain the same. Recognizing this is pivotal.

If you find yourself experiencing the same emotions as before, it is worth delving deeper and exploring which specific behaviors, atmospheres, or moods trigger these emotional states within you. This exploration allows you to gain insight into how the past drama is being repeated in the present.

Ask yourself the following questions: What do I secretly yearn for in this relationship? What do I expect from the other person? Is there any overlap between these expectations and those I had in past relationships? How were my needs met or dismissed in the past? In what ways did the other person keep their distance and prevent true connection? What behaviors, both then and now, foster the hope that one day I will receive the attention you long for? How do you find myself repeatedly disappointed?

Approach this process with a sense of detachment, stepping outside of your emotional perception and observing events with a curious and investigative mindset. Imagine yourself as a diligent researcher seeking to unravel a mystery. Look for clues as to why your relationships and close connections seem to follow similar patterns.

Once you identify who your partner reminds you of, you can delve even deeper to gain a better understanding of your current situation. Consider what you know, and what you don't know, about your past significant other. Reflect on their upbringing, behaviors within your family, and their emotional openness and responsiveness. Did their own history contribute to these qualities?

It is important to note that examining your history and the role of attachment figures may initially be challenging without a neutral perspective. As children, we tend to perceive our parents as all-knowing beings, as we depend on them completely. If something negative happens, we often internalize the blame rather than hold our parents responsible. Recognizing their limitations would mean facing overwhelming helplessness. How could a young child survive with incapable parents? Thus, we view our parents as almost untouchable and blame ourselves for the lack of attention.

This internal dialogue revolves around our perceived deficiencies:

- ♦ not being interesting enough,
- ♦ boring,
- ♦ unlovable,
- ♦ or unpleasant.

We believe that something about us pushes others away

This self-image of flaws and mistakes arises from our tendency to search for faults within ourselves to explain the behavior of others, both in the past and present. As a result, we reinforce and validate this perspective by interpreting thoughtless, un-loving, and critical comments as further confirmation of our inherent defects. Believing that we must try harder to be ac-cepted, we develop a range of behaviors to gain the attention we desire.

We develop a self-image of mistakes by attributing our faults to explain the behavior of others, just as we did in the past with our partners and close caregivers. Consequently, we dis-cover a series of flaws and faults within ourselves that we be-lieve explain our lack of affection. The thoughtless, unloving, and critical comments from others only serve to reinforce and confirm our negative view of ourselves. This reinforces the belief that we must work hard to "fit in" and earn the love we desire. We come to the logical conclusion that if we try hard enough, we will receive the love we want. This leads us to develop a set of behaviors specifically designed to grab the attention of others.

We are convinced that we can only...

- Outdo or outperform our siblings: In adulthood, this belief manifests as clinging, jealousy, attachment, and the constant effort to stand out through exceptional performance.
- Be particularly exciting: As a result, we may be inclined to exaggerate, indulge in vivid imaginations, and attempt to portray our lives as more thrilling and exciting than they actually are.
- Suffer excessively in order to evoke sympathy from others and finally receive attention: This may manifest in the form of self-imposed diseases, adopting a victim mentality, and self-sabotage. We believe that by suffering, we can generate the minimal attention we seek, and being well would threaten that attention.
- Be either loud or quiet enough to either draw attention to ourselves or avoid causing disturbance: In our attempts to gain attention, we may push ourselves into the spotlight or refrain from expressing our needs and emotions. By doing so, we at least receive attention through our listening and giving space to others.

At the core of all these wounds lies the belief that we are fundamentally unlovable and must continually earn affection.

By all means, this strategy proves fruitful at some point or another; otherwise, it would not have been maintained. As children, we received various forms of attention through our experiments, such as:

- Material goods
- Superficial attention without true presence

- Negative attention in the form of criticism, shaming, prohibitions, scolding, and anger
- Ambivalent attention characterized by fluctuating emotional moods
- Attention when we listened to our caregivers
- Attention driven by guilt, but short-lived

What we truly desired was a form of attention that conveyed, "I am delighted to be with you wholeheartedly because you bring me immense joy! There is nothing more beautiful for me right now than being in your presence and showering you with love and affection."

However, the attention we received instead helped us survive but also caused more damage. Essentially, the behavior of our caregivers confirmed our negative beliefs. Through your efforts to stay connected, you may not have experienced the kind of love that truly fulfilled your heart, but at least you were not left completely alone. Today, you may still find yourself operating in a survival mode within your relationships, creating an ideal environment for emotional dependency. This mindset prevents you from developing a sense of safety and security, keeping your inner system in a constant state of stress. You find yourself repeating the strategies of the past, yielding the same unsatisfying outcomes. The result is emotional bondage and a sense of not truly belonging in your relationships and with yourself.

It is crucial to understand that your partner is not solely responsible for what happens and how you feel. This statement is not meant to blame or point fingers at you, but rather to emphasize your capacity for self-efficacy. You have the power to actively change negative experiences in your life because you no longer need to be dependent on the other person. Taking responsibility can be empowering and uplifting when you start to see the first glimpses of success and realize that things can be different.

The more deeply you recognize how you sought care from specific caregivers, the type of care you received as a result, and the parallels between those relationships and your present ones, the more purposefully you can transform your beliefs. It is important to note that you don't have to embark on this journey alone. Many people mistakenly believe that emotional independence means they have to navigate everything independently and that needing someone is always a negative thing. With the best of intentions, they attempt to walk the path of healing alone in order to dissolve emotional dependency. However, this approach only reinforces feelings of loneliness and the negative beliefs associated with it.

Emotional independence is different from the lonely path of complete self-reliance. The goal is to cultivate relationships based on equality, where you can care for yourself and stand up for your needs. It is about recognizing your worth and making choices that are beneficial for your well-being, while creating healing through positive experiences. If we perceive independence as requiring us to be alone and do everything on our own, we are moving away from our inherent human nature. We are profoundly social beings who thrive in communities, seeking loving connections, a sense of belonging, and inner harmony with ourselves and others. Independence, in this sense, is an illusion. We need each other, and that is a beautiful aspect of being human. It is through others that we truly recognize ourselves. This is precisely why the unhealthy attention from our caregivers has such a destructive impact. If we genuinely didn't need each other, everyone could go their separate ways and find happiness independently. However, it is evident that this is not the path to true fulfillment.

We can learn to rediscover our self-worth, to feel it deeply within us, and to draw new conclusions from this realization. *If I am truly valuable, it is only natural that I choose an environment where people treat me in the way I deserve. I learn to express my needs because they are important, and gradually develop the expectation that my loved ones will gladly meet them.*

Inspiration

If you wish, envision what an "ideal childhood" would have been like for you. Imagine that your parents had embraced you with boundless love, openness, and enthusiasm, always being there for you. If this concept feels challenging, allow yourself to entertain the idea of having had different parents who possessed these qualities.

Describe the emotions and the sense of vitality that arises from this imagination. Can you feel the lightness, joy, and zest for life expanding within you? Envision the kind of relationships and the type of partner you would choose if you had grown up with a high standard of care, accustomed to receiving attention, love, affection, and delight in both yourself and life.

What might your life look like today?

And what actions can you take today to gift yourself with this attention?

Remember, in this second step, that immediate change cannot be achieved overnight. It requires taking small steps and seeking professional guidance, therapy, coaching, or counseling to facilitate the transformation. Additionally, nurturing personal relationships in which you can have positive experiences is invaluable. Direct your focus towards these relationships and allow them to flourish. Embrace every opportunity where you encounter experiences different from the negative ones from your childhood. By doing so, you will strengthen a new, positive outlook on life.

Moving Beyond Dependency - Rediscovering Self-Efficacy

To find a way out of emotional dependency, it is essential to explore what you need in order to stop seeking your security solely in another person. Being emotionally dependent means that you have outsourced your resources to someone else.

Visualize the following image in your mind: All the people currently present in your life, the challenges, struggles, fears, and doubts you face are results of your inner beliefs about yourself. Simplistically speaking, you can consider them as products of your own creation. It is important to note here that not everything you experience is always solely your own creation, as some esoteric teachings claim. Many aspects of our lives are beyond our control, and it is not compassionate to blame ourselves for attracting every experience.

What is meant here are the recurring patterns that are part of your inner world and your attitude towards life. Let's consider two examples:

Example:

Annika has spent years searching for her purpose in life. Her favorite pastime involves immersing herself in books, podcasts, courses, and trainings, where she admires individuals who embody the qualities she secretly aspires to possess. However, within her relationship, Annika grapples with the desire to receive more attention from her partner and be truly recognized for who she is at her core.

Over time, Annika realizes that she has been projecting all her resources outward, observing how others live the life she yearns for. The individuals she admires and seeks attention from become integral characters in her inner narrative, shaping her current perception of life. However, none of these people, whose books she avidly reads or videos she watches daily, truly know her or actively invest time to be with her. Her partner, too, remains unaware of the true essence of Annika, as she longs for the qualities exhibited by other individuals who serve as her clients.

Deeply fearful of being truly seen, Annika recognizes that embracing her authentic self and pursuing her heartfelt desires would require dismantling the roles she has assigned to those around her, including the characters she encounters in books. It would mean reclaiming agency and stepping into the leading role of her own life story. However, as a child, Annika was never encouraged to take on this role. She often found herself holding back, lacking the necessary support, and waiting for her parents to prioritize her needs, which seldom occurred. Consequently, Annika internalized the belief that the leading role was not meant for her, despite her longing for it. She gradually lost her innate self-confidence and sought vitality through others, becoming a mere observer and a yearning presence.

Facing this realization, Annika visualizes this inner picture, acknowledging that she has relinquished her self-efficacy while being comfortably nestled on her living room sofa. From this safe and invulnerable space, she could envision the possibilities of an active and fulfilling life without fully immersing herself in the uncomfortable reality of actively pursuing it. She had become addicted to the emotional rush of hearing repeatedly that anything is possible, that she can accomplish anything and is capable of greatness. Consequently, she developed an emotional dependence on the attention of her partner, who gradually grew hesitant in providing it.

Another example:

Maria constantly feels the need to fight for love and attention. She longs for an attentive and devoted partner who recognizes and fulfills her needs. However, based on her past experiences, she consistently chooses partners who seem to do the opposite. Maria often feels lonely and believes she is the only one in the relationship who desires more closeness.

As Maria visualizes the inner picture of her story, she becomes aware that she has adopted the role of the eternal longingly. The people, especially her partners, assume the role that she unconsciously assigns to them, thereby perpetuating the image. In order to remain in her longing role, others continuously run away, or her subconscious choice leads her to individuals who always distance themselves. Maria becomes emotionally dependent on these people because she has relinquished her self-efficacy in favor of their role.

Similar to Annika and Maria, you can also ask yourself: What does the inner picture of my life look like? What role have I taken on, and what roles do others play in my story? Who have I unconsciously imagined them to be? To whom have I surrendered my self-efficacy, dreams, desires, and needs? In what ways have I outsourced and distanced myself from them in order to protect myself? Most importantly, what unconscious benefits do I gain from not asserting my self-efficacy in life? How do I utilize these roles?

As you delve into these questions, you may discover that many of your present and past experiences in relationships are influenced by your co-creation. The roles you assign to yourself and others to confirm your old beliefs may be detrimental to you and your relationships. In surrendering your self-efficacy, you unintentionally contribute to passive roles born out of helplessness, powerlessness, fear, and insecurity. If you do not actively live in a way that serves your well-being, others will take over.

Recognizing where you have yielded control to others and your old patterns is crucial. It is important to reclaim your self-efficacy and reclaim ownership of your experiences. However, this is not an easy task, and it takes time to restructure and implement these changes. You may have spent a significant portion of your life playing various versions of your role. Approach this process with gentleness, thoughtfulness, and understanding for yourself. Rediscovering self-efficacy and breaking free from emotional dependency is a courageous decision. Treat yourself with the same kindness and compassion you would want from others.

This is already the first step towards self-efficacy:

1. Recognize that you desire a change in how others treat you and how you treat yourself.

   Your experiences of emotional dependence stem from your perception of self-worth. Although you yearn for something different, you may find it immensely challenging to allow yourself to pursue that change. Questions may arise: What am I truly capable of? Who am I without my partner? What do I genuinely want to pursue if I no longer shape my life according to the desires of others? If you wish, you can practice observing yourself for a few days: In which moments do you feel powerless and dependent? What triggers a longing gaze from your partner, a denied request, or a hidden longing within you? Can you detach yourself and observe from an external perspective? How would you act if you were not bound by old patterns?

2. Practice expressing your current feelings and emotions.

   This step is crucial in reclaiming an active role in your experiences. Rather than continuously chasing after your partner or fighting vigorously for their attention, or resorting to withdrawing or controlling behaviors, communicate your emotions honestly.

   "For some reason, I have the urge to ask you who you're spending time with today—I feel afraid that you might be turning away from me and finding someone else more appealing."

"I'm on the verge of tears right now, and I have the thought that if only you would chase after me and take care of me, I could let go. I need..."

"I feel completely at the mercy of your coldness. I become stiff in your presence and remain silent, yet deep down, I long to be enveloped in your arms."

Initially, your needs may not be fully met during this initial period of change. Therefore, instead of focusing solely on the outcome or expecting others to change, concentrate on summoning the courage to gradually transform your own role. When you change, the situation changes because you play an instrumental part in shaping it.

3. Delve deeply into the fears that hinder you from stepping into your self-efficacy.

What are you afraid of? What fears have you been evading throughout your life? Some individuals who have become emotionally dependent fear being alone and receiving no attention whatsoever if they become more independent. Others fear failure and making mistakes. Still, others are terrified of confronting uncomfortable conflicts, as the deeper fear of rejection looms large. What about you? What does emotional dependence shield you from? What is it that you lack the courage to do, expecting the other person to do it for you?

4. Equip yourself with a resource kit.

Often, our fears stem from feeling inadequate because we lack the confidence to acquire the skills necessary for our self-assurance. By ensuring our resource box is well-stocked, we can confront many of these fears. Reclaim or cultivate the resources and skills we project onto others. Self-efficacy involves confronting life with our entire being, showing up fully present and vulnerable. This is what people mean when they say, "We love in others what we lack in ourselves, and would be everything, but what we are." Emotional dependency acts as a hiding place—a refuge—but for what purpose? Here's an example of what your resource kit might include:

- The ability to empathize: You possess a particular skill for connecting with and understanding others. Consider developing this ability further and learning how to effectively communicate it.

- Embracing strong emotions: Feelings like anger can serve as powerful tools for building strength and self-efficacy. When you genuinely allow yourself to experience anger in moments where things don't go your way, it can become a driving force for initiating change. Train yourself to honor this feeling, rather than suppressing it. Take a deep breath and reflect on what this feeling is trying to convey and what changes it may require. Our emotions offer valuable insights into what is beneficial or detrimental to us.

- ◆ Education and knowledge: It is not uncommon to feel incapable in relationships or various aspects of our lives due to a lack of relevant knowledge and experience that would make us feel more confident or knowledgeable. Many individuals find themselves oscillating between undesirable situations because they lack an understanding of what is truly transpiring. Our personal perspectives can be limited, and occasionally, we need a fresh outlook and further education to better comprehend ourselves and our relationships. Seek support and opportunities that shed light on the unknown.

- ◆ Wholehearted engagement: Many individuals, out of self-preservation, withhold certain aspects of themselves from the healing process. They ignore certain realities, avoid confronting daily life, immerse themselves in idealized visions of the future, or seek distractions. By not fully engaging with the present, they miss out on truly experiencing their emotions and the current reality. By immersing yourself fully in the present moment, you can authentically acknowledge what is truly occurring. Although this may involve confronting pain that you have skillfully evaded, it also provides an opportunity to firmly say "no" and make change inevitable. Self-efficacy emerges when we adjust the right levers that facilitate the necessary change. Until we are truly present, our energy disperses in various directions, and we lack agency. Gradually train yourself to be fully present and genuinely attuned to the current moment.

♦ Nurturing relationships: Relationships serve as resources that support your journey. Surround yourself with individuals who encourage you, speak highly of you, accept you as you are, and provide attention and friendship. These relationships strengthen your self-efficacy. Often, good friends remind us of our self-worth and demonstrate the beauty of connecting with others on an equal footing. Especially within emotionally dependent relationships, it is vital to experience yourself in different connections, ones that offer an entirely different dynamic and bring you closer to your authentic self. Continuously realize and remind yourself that your current relationship dynamic does not define normal. It is not about criticizing your partner or yourself but rather about recognizing untapped potential, acknowledging your multifaceted nature, and realizing the value of cultivating independence and a deeper connection with yourself within the relationship. Many individuals become trapped in tunnel vision, only perceiving their dependent structures, losing courage, and experiencing suffering. Good friends help you gain an alternative perspective on yourself and prompt you to step out of your story through different experiences. Suddenly, you may realize that your emotional dependency feels like a movie from which you can extricate yourself, providing a tremendous boost to your newfound self-efficacy.

Inspiration

Prepare your resource kit!

Here, you will find areas to consider when assembling your resource kit:

Emotional Resources:
Identify the emotions you wish to experience and harness more frequently.

Social Resources:
List the names of individuals who positively impact your well-being and with whom you desire to spend more time in the future.

Action Skills:
Reflect on your existing strengths and interests. What activities do you enjoy? Additionally, identify areas where you would like to further develop your skills.

Self-Care:
Determine what brings you strength, relaxation, encouragement, and overall well-being.

Health:
Consider how you can prioritize your health. What specific physical resources do you already possess? How can you adjust your diet to improve your fitness, balance, and overall well-being?

Letting Go of Old Habits

Emotional dependence is often accompanied by various detrimental habits that reinforce feelings of inadequacy, incapacity, and low self-worth. By harming ourselves through these habits, we inadvertently validate our negative beliefs and perpetuate the cycle of dependency. Some unhealthy habits to be aware of include:

- Addictions: Introducing harmful substances such as alcohol, drugs, cigarettes, and others to fulfill a deep inner need is an unhealthy habit. Exploring the underlying reasons for these addictions would require a more in-depth discussion. In summary, it comes down to making an important decision:

  "I'm letting go of habits that don't benefit me because I'm choosing what I truly want." However, breaking free from addictive habits requires more than this realization. If you desire assistance on this journey, seeking competent guidance is recommended.

- Unhealthy Sleep Patterns: Maintaining a healthy sleep rhythm is essential for processing experiences, resting, and facilitating personal growth. Emotionally dependent individuals often find themselves consumed by their relationships, with racing thoughts and heightened emotions following them into their nighttime hours. You may be familiar with periods when getting adequate rest was challenging, as you stayed up late browsing social media or struggled to distance yourself from pain and challenges, hindering your ability to relax and fall asleep.

Setting rules for yourself, particularly during times of crisis, can help you navigate the challenging period of change effectively. Consider putting away all electronic devices at least an hour before bedtime, avoiding coffee and preferably alcohol in the evening, and establishing a habit of engaging in a short evening meditation or practicing deep and conscious breathing for two to three minutes. Focus on feeling your body and arriving in the present moment. Additionally, strive to maintain a regular sleep schedule, being mindful of the number of hours of sleep you personally require and setting goals to achieve that level.

If you find yourself in a stressful relationship, it's worth contemplating whether you can and want to occasionally sleep alone, especially if the relationship is strained. This can provide you with some space at night to reconnect with yourself.

Adequate and undisturbed sleep can enhance your brain function, provide easier access to your emotions, and enable you to work more consciously on changing your situation. Reshaping your life requires energy, which can be fostered through quality sleep.

- Excessive or Unhealthy Media Consumption: Many individuals seek refuge in imaginary worlds or use media as a distraction. Excessive consumption of television, the internet, and other media platforms that offer little substance can disconnect us from our bodies, inhibit self-awareness, and leave us feeling negative emotions such as guilt and a lack of vitality, presence, and activity. This behavior reinforces our inner beliefs and perpetuates the negative cycle, keeping us emotionally dependent on others. By not dedicating our time to living in a way that aligns with our personal well-being and fosters a renewed zest for life, we remain trapped in this cycle.

To initiate change, it's crucial to create periods of time when external influences are minimized. While we often believe that exposure to more external input, learning from others' actions, and seeking inspiration—often facilitated by the vast possibilities of the internet—will lead to a solution tailored to our situation, the truth is that no one is in the exact same circumstances as us, and no one can make decisions or change our lives for us. We require space to fully experience and acknowledge our pain, recognizing when it's time to change direction.

- Nutrition: To cultivate the energy needed to forge a path forward, it is vital to provide optimal support to your body. Your feelings manifest in the body, affecting your memory, warning systems, and protective mechanisms. All of these aspects are now undergoing a transformation, including the development of new habits, beliefs, and attitudes toward life. Your body may resist this change in various ways, creating the impression that things are moving in the wrong direction as it tries to protect you. Despite aiming for positive

change, your body is accustomed to different circumstances due to past experiences and seeks to maintain
the familiar. Consequently, changing direction requires
substantial energy and awareness. To facilitate this process, it is beneficial to nourish your body with healthy,
nutrient-rich foods. This approach contrasts with sub-
jecting your body to additional stress through an unhealthy detoxification process.

Draw Conclusions

Once you have taken steps to establish a sense of security and
a positive outlook by changing your habits, it is important to
objectively evaluate your current situation. Reflect on the following questions:

- ◆ How do you want to feel in a relationship?
  It is crucial to accurately describe your desired emotional state. People become more attentive when addressed on an emotional level. Remember that feelings are
  significant to our souls. Examples of desired feelings
  include security, safety, contentment, inspiration, value,
  and loveability.

- ◆ How do you currently feel about your relationship?

  Be honest, objective, and avoid embellishment. Try not
  to attribute your partner's feelings to yourself or describe the situation in a way that makes you responsible
  for those emotions. Embrace and acknowledge your

negative feelings as they are, recognizing that they belong to you. You may feel tired, worn out, discouraged, worthless, sad, hopeless, lonely, under pressure, dull, or annoyed.

- How long have you been feeling this way? What recurring thoughts provide you with a sense of perspective about your situation?

Examples:

"Oh, that will change soon."

"I'm on a good path after all! My partner and I can do this together."

"He's working on himself, isn't he? I just need a little more patience."

"He just can't help himself. He had a difficult childhood. Together we will heal."

"If I break up, I'm going to go through the same thing again with a new partner anyway."

Take note of the deep-seated patterns that have influenced your thoughts and behaviors for years, extending beyond your current relationship. It's important to also pay attention to your partner's fundamental qualities. Reflect on what qualities initially attracted you to them and consider any unexpected behaviors or dynamics that emerged as the relationship progressed. Compare these dynamics to past experiences, particularly those you hoped to avoid in this relationship. Lastly, evaluate the level of commitment your partner is demonstrating in creating positive change alongside you.

- ◆ Truth: Have a conversation with your partner about your observations, fears, and prospects for the future based on your dynamics together. Clearly express that you do not want to continue as things are. Share how you have recognized emotionally dependent patterns within yourself and express your desire to overcome them. Be open to your partner joining you on this journey, but also be receptive to the possibility that this path may not align with your partner's intentions.

Based on your findings, draw conclusions and take appropriate actions. These consequences may vary, but their effectiveness lies in your honesty with yourself. Consider the following possibilities:

Working together on the relationship: This approach is viable when both partners share the same goal and can clearly articulate their respective contributions to improving the relationship. For emotionally dependent individuals, this step can be challenging as they often assume their partner's responsibilities to keep the process moving. Old beliefs, such as "I'm not deserving of anyone's care" or "I always have to do everything on my own," become active. It is crucial for emotionally dependent individuals to be honest with themselves. Assess whether your partner is making measurable efforts to improve the relationship. Do their words align with their actions, or do you find yourself constantly reminding them of their responsibilities? Assess whether you can rely on your partner's word without having to push them.

Separation within the relationship: Discuss together the idea of creating some distance between each other for a certain period of time to give yourselves a break. This option can be particularly challenging if you are emotionally dependent, as you may find yourself constantly rationalizing staying in the relationship even when positive change seems unlikely. It's important to consider separation within the relationship only if both partners share the goal of reconnecting and see a potential for continuing the shared path in the future. Alternatively, you can make this decision independently to focus on your own self-development and let go of preconceived notions about the future of the relationship. It's crucial to be aware of a common thought process that arises from emotional dependence: "I choose separation within the relationship so that my relationship still has a chance." However, this often means that the decision is not truly for oneself, but driven by beliefs and the desire for the partner to love more when one becomes more independent. Therefore, separation within the relationship should genuinely aim at rediscovering oneself and embracing self-love unconditionally.

Final separation: This step becomes necessary when you feel that you cannot find a way out of emotional dependence together with your partner, and over time, more energy is being depleted while pain and hurt continue to multiply. Final separation is warranted in the following situations:

1. The partner exhibits strong narcissistic personality traits that hinder a healthy exchange and prevent striving for equality. This occurs when the partner fails to recognize the need for personal growth and self-improvement.
2. You realize that severing ties is necessary to constructively address the structures of your emotional dependency.
3. Both of you have exhausted all available options that seemed beneficial, yet you recognize that you are fundamentally incompatible or no longer compatible.
4. You reach a point where you no longer desire the relationship. Even individuals experiencing emotional dependence eventually arrive at a moment when they close their hearts. They recognize their inherent worth and decide to embark on a fresh start, wholeheartedly saying yes to themselves, which entails letting go of the old, including the relationship.

Inspiration

That's enough!

Take the time to familiarize yourself with your personal boundary. Connect with your inner self during this process:

What do you desire for yourself and your relationship? How do you envision the experience of living with yourself and others?

Contrast that with your current reality. How would you describe your relationship with yourself and others? How long are you willing to continue living in this way?

Imagine being stuck in this situation a year from now, two years from now, or three years from now. How does that make you feel?

Try to tap into your sense of how long you are willing to hold onto hope or strive for change within the existing circumstances. Once you reach a conclusion, fully embrace and acknowledge it! If you feel you can endure for another year, consider what proactive steps you can take this year to initiate the change and healing from emotional dependency. Don't let this year slip away. Remember that it requires active action, as simply hoping for others to take action is unlikely to yield results.

If it resonates with you, you can symbolically mark the time period and your commitment to invest further with a metaphorical red line:

Up to this point and no further. This is where I draw the line. This is where I put an end to the situation.
I no longer allow my partner to... I am going to stop...

Be mindful of not setting the red line solely with your mind, but with your emotions as well. Where does the red line truly lie? Do you wish you had set it earlier? How does the red line feel to you? Does asserting your own boundaries scare you? What fears and bodily sensations arise when you envision the red line in your mind? What are the consequences of saying no? What lies on the other side of the red line?

Accompaniment

To break free from emotional dependency, you have access to various sources of beneficial professional support. Therapy or seeking treatment in a clinic are options if you are already experiencing burnout, depression, or other severe symptoms. Another choice is to engage with a well-trained coach as a companion or take a longer break in a different location. It is also beneficial to examine other aspects of your life: How is your job affecting you? Does it contribute positively to your well-being or does it further drain you? What about your relationships? Do you have friendships that are nourishing and beneficial?

It's important to note that the current market in this field is flourishing. Many individuals offer psychological coaching without possessing a solid education. There are numerous models being promoted primarily to attract and persuade clients, resulting in financial gain for the coach. To distinguish reputable offers, consider whether it is a series of cheap deals that eventually transform into costly proposals or if the coach has verifiable training, demonstrating genuine expertise acquired through practical application, not just theory.

Determining the most suitable form of therapy can be achieved through discussions with your doctor, while in a clinic, or by consulting different therapists. Take your time when selecting a therapist who is the right fit for you: ensure that you feel a connection with them and that you can establish genuine trust. The therapeutic relationship between the therapist and client is crucial for a successful therapy with positive outcomes.

For additional information on this subject, the book „Even Old Wounds Can Heal" by Dami Charf provides valuable insights.

Chapter 5
Embracing Self-Worth

"To love oneself is the beginning of a lifelong romance."

Oscar Wilde

As we delve into the journey of self-discovery and empowerment, it is essential to recognize our inherent worth. Perhaps you have come to realize, during the process of assembling your resource bag, that cultivating and expanding the resources that enable personal growth is not always a straightforward task. What could be the underlying reason for this challenge? One crucial factor is closely intertwined with our self-esteem. Do we truly believe that we deserve to let go of old, detrimental habits? Are we uncertain about standing up for ourselves, questioning our worthiness to pursue well-being and satisfaction?

Rediscovering and embracing our self-worth takes time. Be kind and patient with yourself, allowing space to acknowledge the areas and ways in which your self-worth has been undermined and wounded. Where have you allowed others to diminish your sense of worth? In what ways do you perpetuate self-deprecation? How do you speak to yourself and treat yourself? Reflect upon whether you would tolerate someone else speaking to you in such a manner. Additionally, consider the actions you engage in that contribute to diminishing your self-worth.

Recognizing Your Self-Worth

In our everyday lives, we can easily identify even the smallest, inconspicuous actions that influence our self-esteem. How do you respond when you experience a physical need such as hunger, thirst, cold, heat, the desire for touch, comfort, or relief? Do you prioritize these needs and attend to them promptly and lovingly? Or do you tend to tense up and endure, suppressing your needs when they arise?

Now, consider your emotional needs. How do you handle feelings of loneliness? Do you reach out to an old flame? Do you spend time with people who uplift you and make you feel good, or do you seek distractions to avoid experiencing those emotions? Can you identify and communicate your needs to others in a way that they can understand and meet them? Many individuals with emotional dependency seek fulfillment from people who, for various reasons, are unable or unwilling to meet those desires. This pattern often leads to unhappy relationships. We unconsciously choose partners who possess the same qualities as those who were absent in our significant others in the past. For example, you may have a need to share your deepest thoughts, but your partner is unable to provide the space you require. Instead of reaching out to a close friend, you feel resentful towards your partner for not meeting your needs, perpetuating the cycle of dependency.

Take Note:

If you blame your partner or others for not fulfilling your needs, your self-esteem will suffer. You will repeatedly feel unworthy of receiving voluntary attention and believe that you must force it from others. Recognizing this is crucial because we often believe that to enhance our self-worth, we must assertively communicate it to those around us. However, this approach conveys the opposite message. It is beneficial to detach your self-worth from the actions and attitudes of others and remind yourself that *you are inherently valuable, independent of external validation.*

- ✦ What can you do today to positively impact your self-esteem?
- ✦ What have you been yearning for that you can incorporate into your plans this week?
- ✦ What truths have been left unspoken in your partnership for a long time?
- ✦ How can you attend to your physical needs today in a way that reaffirms your importance and value in your own body?

*

Now, let's explore different areas of your life to identify potential opportunities for strengthening your self-worth.

Note: It is important to approach this task with a positive mindset. If you focus on areas where you perceive a lack of self-worth, it may bring your mood down. However, by shifting your focus to positive development, you will uplift your emotional state and gain the motivation to view your life in a brighter light.

Here are some helpful approaches and inspiration:

- Reflect on your social connections and identify an acquaintance who is not beneficial for your well-being. Decide how you want to address this to strengthen your self-worth: Would you like to have a clarifying conversation? Do you need to confront them? Do you want to share your feelings? Is ending the contact the best option? Consider what would bring you relief and align with your inner truth.

- Similarly, choose a contact that is good for you and approach it in a similar way: How can you nurture and develop this relationship? Would you like to express your feelings to that person? Do you want to engage in specific activities together or spend more time with them? How about setting aside a dedicated day to prioritize each other? Communicate your desires openly, with curiosity and approachability. You may be pleasantly surprised by the positive feedback you receive.

- Consider incorporating a new habit into your daily routine. Do you yearn to start the day alone and in peace? How much time would you like to allocate? Is there a particular activity such as reading, hiking, or something else that you wish to engage in more regularly? Can you identify an existing habit that you can replace with a new one that better serves you?

- Reflect on any substitute gratifications you have developed in your life that prevent you from actively pursuing what you truly desire. Do you find yourself escaping from reality, longing to be somewhere else, or daydreaming instead of taking active, realistic steps towards change? Is fantasizing about possibilities a substitute for fulfillment? How much do you yearn to wake up in the morning and step into another reality, and what practical steps can you take in the next three days to replace the dream with actual actions in the present?

- Create a wish list of ten desires that you have been putting on hold because they may seem unrealistic in your current reality. If it feels right to you, share these wishes with someone close to you and express how much you would like to bring them to fruition. Ask if they are willing to support you mentally or even actively participate. Let them know that you seek positive encouragement to do something meaningful for yourself. In our fast-paced, individual-oriented times, genuine connections with others have become rare. We listen to motivational speakers who don't know us personally, while our friends remain unaware of our true aspirations. We confide in our journals, but our partners are left in the dark because we don't truly expect them to understand or care about our needs.

> *At this point, ask yourself the following question:*
>
> *Who is your partner? Who are your friends? Are you truly being authentic and showing your true self to them?*

- Allow yourself to imagine what it is like to live in alignment with your true worth. Focus particularly on your immediate environment. While it's common to have grand dreams to showcase our self-worth, the reality is often shaped by our everyday lives, habits, and close relationships. Take a brief inner journey and visualize a daily life where your needs and positive aspects of your personality take center stage in your personal life.

- Identify your actions or decisions that have been long overdue. What have you been postponing for weeks, months, or even years? How would it feel to finally take action? What sense of freedom would arise from taking that step?

- Reflect on what it means to follow your own path. How does this concept apply to your work, relationships, and everyday life? Break down this question into smaller, manageable areas: How can you make your work day more relaxed? Are there gradual steps you can take to work less? Would a career change be beneficial? How can you foster different dynamics in your interactions with employees, colleagues, and superiors?

Envision your ideal mornings and afternoons. How can you assert your personal path during weekends

- Ask yourself: "Who actually says that I am not valuable, and where does my conviction come from to accept that this person is right? How can I choose to believe in my own value and see that statement as truth?" Treat this as a creative exercise that involves contemplation, writing, and grappling with the weight you assign to statements and words about yourself. You will begin to realize that you have the power to determine which statements hold significance, whose advice you listen to, and what truly matters to you personally.

- Self-esteem also stems from trusting yourself to make sound choices and embracing the freedom to live life on your own terms as an adult. Many individuals who experience emotional dependence have never encountered the trust of their caregivers, nor the validation that their impulses, ideas, and curiosity can guide them in a positive direction. However, today you can bestow upon yourself the trust that may have been withheld in the past. Allow your ideas to expand! Embrace creativity and enjoyment, and follow your impulses as long as they do not have a lasting negative impact on others. The aim is to rekindle joy in your own life and ideas. Lessening emotional dependence involves reducing the need for external validation or permission when making decisions that shape your own life.

I Am Worthy Of...

...being with people who genuinely want to be with me.

This realization can be difficult for many individuals who experience emotional dependence. What does it truly mean to feel that someone genuinely enjoys having you around?

- ◆ They care about your well-being. Someone who truly loves you is attentive to how their behavior affects your well-being. They take responsibility for their actions towards you and don't disregard your needs.

- ◆ They enjoy spending time with you without seeking benefits that drain you. This means that they value you and your presence, and they aren't using you as a means to fill emotional voids or simply make themselves feel better. They are ready to meet you as equals because you hold significance to them from the depths of their heart.

- ◆ They prioritize you without having to fight for it. They take the initiative to spend time with you, set aside space and time for you, and actively contribute to shaping the relationship. They prioritize you over less important matters and say no to other things in order to preserve the space you share.

- ◆ They follow through on agreements. When they make a promise, it stems from intrinsic motivation, and it matters to them to keep that promise. They are not driven solely by fear of upsetting or disappointing you, but rather by their genuine desire to do something good for you and because your relationship holds importance to them.

- ◆ They consider your viewpoints and opinions in their decision-making process regarding your life together, without feeling swayed or manipulated. This means that they value your perspective as much as their own. You can observe this in their willingness to engage in open communication about your point of view or their clear expression of interest in your opinion without downplaying or dismissing it.

...letting go when I am not being held.

What does it mean to be held in a healthy way in adulthood? Isn't the longing for it something childlike?

No, on the contrary. We all need to be held by another person from time to time. It is not only childlike, but also a fundamental human need. We all find ourselves in difficult moments when support from others brings us solace. This doesn't mean that we relinquish responsibility, but rather that we deserve to expect others to accompany and support us as we navigate our own journeys. We still carry the responsibility ourselves, make decisions, and take action. However, in these moments, we can pour out our hearts to others, receive their embrace, and find reassurance that we are not alone. If your partner or another person fundamentally refuses this companionship and resists offering loving emotional and physical support, it may be worth considering letting go. The need for support is human and healthy. No one should make you feel guilty about seeking it or insinuate that you are incapable of managing on your own.

...being the center of my own life.

This means prioritizing your own needs before attending to the needs of others. It is not selfish or negative to focus on yourself, but rather an act of self-care. Only when you are well can you effectively care for others. If you are particularly empathetic and outward-focused, it is natural for you to care for others. However, the path to yourself is often neglected, and you may gradually let go of any guilt associated with prioritizing your own well-being first.

How can you tell that you are no longer the center of your own life?

- ◆ *When you feel emotionally controlled by others:* The people around us have an influence on us, whether we acknowledge it or not. Science has discovered that our mirror neurons enable us to recognize and experience ourselves in others, and vice versa. Therefore, it's not entirely true that we can live our lives completely independent of other people. It's important to be aware that those who are close to us have an impact on our perception, emotional state, and even our thoughts. Consequently, we co-create situations together. Understanding this can help you comprehend why you may feel differently in the presence of different individuals. Choose to spend time with people who uplift and make you feel good about yourself. This doesn't mean you have to avoid all uncomfortable feelings or confrontation, but there is a distinct difference between being lovingly challenged and consciously addressing your shadows, and being belittled, diminished, and bullied by others. Manipulation also falls into the latter category: Do you often feel confused, disconnected from yourself, and prone to losing your inner clarity around a particular person? If so, it's time to create space for yourself and reflect on how distancing yourself can help you regain clarity.

◆ *If you constantly relativize, delay, or change decisions to please another person:* Deep down, you know what you want and need, don't you? In that regard, how do you feel about the person you are emotionally dependent on? Are they increasingly making decisions about your life, the direction you take, and how you live, in ways that may not align with your desires? Do you often feel that what you truly want doesn't matter at all? Are you constantly making compromises that leave you feeling uneasy? Is there something else you truly desire?

◆ *If the other person rarely shows genuine interest in how you are truly doing:* When was the last time you received undivided attention and felt truly seen and heard? Reflect on this question in the context of all your relationships: How much time do you spend with others during the week, and how much of that time is dedicated to your well-being and nurturance? Do you sense an imbalance? Are you giving more than receiving? Do you feel tired and drained? Do you tend to prioritize others' needs over your own? What underlying need drives your constant concern for others' well-being? Do you feel that someone genuinely cares about you as well? If you sense sadness, resignation, anger, or disappointment, allow yourself to feel these emotions if you can. Tune into your inner self: Where do these feelings manifest in your body? How are you truly feeling? Can you give yourself the attention and care you desire from others for a few moments? How would it feel to reclaim your position as the center of your own life?

◆ *When you spend most of your time trying to keep things going:* Emotionally dependent individuals excel at ensuring that everything runs smoothly. They focus on making others happy, stay constantly busy, often maintain packed schedules, and rarely realize that most of what they do doesn't truly align with their own deepest desires. This behavior stems from childhood, where a sense of not being important was overshadowed by busyness for others.

How does this behavior manifest in your life? What variations of it can you identify within yourself? Do you find activities in your schedule that truly resonate with you? For whom are you doing all that you do?

...allowing myself to feel.

Which feelings, intuitions, and thoughts have you been consistently pushing away? Where are you avoiding them? What would an act of self-love look like in this area?

Take a moment to deeply explore within yourself. Can you perceive a space that can only be felt through focused attention? It is a space that is uniquely accessible to you, where you can understand and experience yourself without the need for effort or change. What would it be like to fully embrace and experience all the emotions that need to be felt? These are your feelings, this is your life. Every new day is filled with breaths, with your body inhaling and exhaling. It is within your body that your feelings arise. What would it be like to allow them, to truly let them be? How would your life change if you allowed the things you try to hide to be present? How would the people around you perceive you if they were given the opportunity to witness what truly moves you? Would unhealthy symbiotic relationships still remain as they are? What if it became more important for you to feel everything and be in tune with yourself, rather than prioritizing the preservation of a relationship or sacrificing your own well-being?

If you wish, take a moment to write down the feelings you have been ignoring or trying to avoid for a long time. Is it loneliness? Shame? Anger? Powerlessness? Helplessness? Determination? And how do you typically respond to or navigate these emotions? Is it through fickleness? Anger? Fatigue? Sabotage? Self-pity? Condemnation?

Inspiration

In order to gain clarity about your current position in relation to emotional dependency, you can create a visual representation. Begin by drawing a large circle that encompasses all the factual aspects of your life right now: your relationship, specific emotions, commitments, people, and circumstances.

Next, draw a symbol at another point on the paper. This symbol represents the place you truly want to reach, the state you long for in your life and relationship. Take note of the distance between this symbol and the large circle that represents your current circumstances. Is the symbol located within the circle, previously unnoticed by you? Or is it far beyond the edge of the paper?

How does it feel to perceive the symbol as intangibly distant from your current reality? Does acknowledging this distance bring it closer in any way? How can you cultivate a deeper connection with what you genuinely desire?

Remember:
Your feelings serve as a guide. Embrace them instead of avoiding them. Allow yourself to feel everything that needs to be felt—the frustration, disappointment, sadness, and longing.

Chapter 6
My Independent Self

*"Our wishes are presentiments of the abilities that lie in us,
harbingers of what we will be able to accomplish."*

Johann Wolfgang von Goethe

E motional dependence involves merging and blending
with another person's being. As human beings, we
naturally yearn for unity and oneness, as it harkens
back to our origins. However, we also possess a fundamental
need for freedom and autonomy. We strive to develop and
explore our individual selves, independent of others. When
this need is compromised due to fear of abandonment and
excessive attachment to others, emotional dependency arises,
leading to unhealthy symbiotic relationships. The distinction
between "me" and "you" becomes blurred and indistinguish-
able. In couples who embrace both closeness and freedom,
and maintain a relationship of equality, this boundary between
individuals may occasionally blur at certain points. However,
both partners are capable of preserving their autonomy and
living fulfilling lives as separate entities, independent of one
another.

Emotional dependency serves as an indicator that our healthy
autonomy has been compromised by past wounds. Therefore,
it is crucial to delve into how we can rediscover and nurture

our innate need for autonomy and freedom, while simultaneously healing our attachment wounds. Through this process, emotional dependency can gradually dissolve, allowing us to find a sense of security and inner home within ourselves.

Who Am I When I Am Not in a Relationship? Who Am I Without Others?

The question of where our boundaries lie and where others begin can be examined from various perspectives. It is important to note that the answer is not as straightforward as it may initially appear.

Since we are significantly influenced, even shaped, by our environment, and we develop differently as soon as we come into contact with external stimuli, we cannot definitively and permanently say, "This is me. This is who I am." We possess a unique personality, and many aspects of ourselves remain with us to varying degrees throughout our eventful lives. However, we always have the opportunity to rediscover and get to know ourselves anew.

When asking the question "Who am I?", it is therefore beneficial not to rely solely on external circumstances or assume that we already know ourselves well enough based on a few quirks and idiosyncrasies. Everything is in a constant state of motion: our bodies are constantly changing, our habits evolve, and our interests and abilities transform. Therefore, instead of clinging to what we know about ourselves, it is important to anchor ourselves within our own being. What does that mean?

Above all, it means genuinely connecting with ourselves as often as possible. The easiest way to achieve this is through our feelings and our bodies. Many individuals who experience emotional dependence struggle to remain connected with themselves when in the presence of others. Some report that they can relax and truly feel themselves better when they are alone.

This act of "feeling yourself" is the pathway, the foundation for answering the question: Who am I when I am not in a relationship? Take a moment to sense within yourself when you are in a relaxed state, free from stress, and at peace. How do you feel? How does your body feel? What sense of vitality do you perceive? How are you?

This question can be approached in three ways:

- *How* are you?
  How do you navigate through the world? How do you typically approach challenges, make decisions, and fulfill your needs? How do you experience yourself in everyday life? Find six to ten adjectives that capture how you feel about yourself. It is also helpful to ask trusted friends how they perceive you.

- How *are* you?
  How do you experience yourself when you are not focused on doing, but simply being? What sensations arise within your body when you are fully present in

the moment, immersed in the experience of being? Describe this through colors, shapes, words, or perhaps create a sculpture that represents your essence as you perceive it. Depict what lies beyond your neuroses and idiosyncrasies, that which exists on a deeper level, beneath the surface.

♦ How are *you*?

What do you believe defines your unique self? How do you recognize yourself, and how do others recognize that it is you? This encompasses character traits as well as your passions, dislikes, chosen social environment, what brings you joy, what hurts you, and what astonishes you. Your sense of self is your ego, the aspect of your being that primarily guides you through everyday life. It is not something negative that needs to be eradicated, as some spiritual teachings suggest. It is a part of your being that anchors you here on earth and is continuously evolving through your experiences and interactions with the world. The ego is a component of your self, your essence, and you do yourself a great favor by befriending and embracing it, along with all your endearing idiosyncrasies.

What are you like? This question is easier to grasp than the question "Who are you?" The way you express yourself, experience yourself, and navigate through the world can be observed both by yourself and others, making it more tangible than the deeper question of identity, which operates on a meta-level and can easily cause confusion.

So, what are you like when you are not heavily influenced by a partner or another person, when they are not occupying your attention, time, and energy?

And let's consider the practical aspects as well:

- What truly matters to you when you are not being influenced by others' opinions of what should be important or significant?
- What hobbies do you pursue when you have the freedom to choose for yourself?
- What motivates you to get off the couch when there are no external demands?
- With which friends do you genuinely enjoy spending time without seeking anything in return that you can't find within yourself? With whom do you truly have fun?
- Are you more introverted or extroverted? How do you typically cope with shyness? Do you become quiet or particularly outgoing?
- Do you enjoy traveling, or do you prefer the cozy comforts of home?
- ...

Inspiration

You may be surprised by how many aspects of yourself are not easily identifiable. It becomes evident when observing how your habits and behaviors change in dependent relationships. That's why it is crucial to observe yourself when you are in a state of freedom. Additionally, you may discover that you channel all your energy into seeking a new attachment opportunity as soon as you find yourself alone.

If you'd like, you can visually represent this concept by creating a sketch on a sheet of paper. Draw a circle to represent yourself, choosing a size that resonates with you. Then, add other circles to the paper that correspond in size and distance to the connections you frequently engage in. Does your circle attach to other circles? Are there circles within your circle? Are you inside other circles? Consider whether you are content with the current arrangement. Do you feel a sense of emptiness when there are no circles within your own?

Create additional profiles of how you perceive yourself in various emotional states when you are not in attached relationships:

- When I am relaxed, my behavior is...
- When I'm under stress, I tend to...
- When I'm sad, this is how I cope:...
- If I am cheerful, it is evident in...
- When faced with time pressure...
- With a free daily routine...
- ...

Take a moment to reflect on how your behavior differs when influenced by emotional dependence. Now, let's delve deeper:

Write down the qualities that the person you feel dependent on must possess in order to disrupt your equilibrium and sense of self. What charisma do they exude? How do they behave? What character traits do they possess? How do they treat you? Describe your experiences in detail, including how they impact your body, emotions, and behavior.

Consider where you may have encountered similar experiences in your childhood. Can you identify any parallels? These insights are invaluable because they help you recognize that your tendencies toward emotional dependence may not be inherent, but rather triggered and activated by specific individuals and circumstances rooted in your personal history. It is likely that you will experience yourself differently, freer, more relaxed, and more connected to your authentic self with individuals who do not reinforce these patterns. This realization offers hope and a broader perspective for self-observation. Remember, being emotionally dependent does not define you exclusively; you are multifaceted.

You are also different.

You are also ...

Write a poem, a text, or a list that highlights who you are, emphasizing the many dimensions of your being beyond emotional dependence. You are so much more—expansive and abundant—than can be captured by that label alone. Embrace this realization to cultivate a positive sense of self-worth and recognize that you are a unique individual separate from any emotionally dependent or toxic connection. It is essential to strengthen this understanding, reconnect with your true self, and befriend yourself. By doing so, you bring your center back to your own core, rather than placing it solely within another person or relationship, allowing you to regain internal balance, resilience, and energetic harmony.

Who Am I in a Relationship When I Stay True to Myself?

After exploring how you feel about yourself (the feeling that reveals "this is me when I'm embracing relaxation and the joy of life"), the next step is to understand the version of yourself that shows up in a relationship. Ideally, you'll find that the same authentic self you embody when you're alone remains intact in your relationships. This means feeling like yourself, without distortion or compromise. You are clear and connected with yourself, able to effectively express your needs and meet others on an equal footing.

Nevertheless, some adjustments in behavior are natural and necessary when engaging in the joint creation of future perspectives, everyday life, and interaction with others. This chapter provides valuable inspiration and support on how to navigate this process.

Stay Connected with Yourself

How can you maintain a strong connection with yourself during communication, sharing, and spending time with another person?

The most effective way is through your body. Continuously bring your attention back to your body, paying attention to your breath, physical sensations, and the messages your body conveys about your present state.

Reconnecting with your body is a profound and ongoing journey. Often, mindfulness exercises reveal how much we are caught up in our thoughts and mental processes in our daily lives. We lose touch with our emotions, sensations, and our bodily awareness. Identifying with your body does not mean constantly striving to appear attractive or seeking recognition, attention, and affirmation solely based on external appearances. It means experiencing yourself as a physical being and being able to recognize and fully inhabit the range of feelings that arise within the body.

Your body serves as an anchor, grounding you in this world and facilitating your interactions with other living beings. By living within your body, you can foster a stronger connection with yourself and learn to differentiate between your own feelings and those attributable to the other person. For individuals struggling with emotional dependence, this can be an initial step toward detachment. Emotionally dependent individuals often prioritize the feelings of others over their own. While this ability was crucial for survival during childhood, it becomes ineffective and destructive when carried into adult relationships, as it involves neglecting one's own needs and emotions to maintain the relationship.

Allocate a few minutes each day to practice tuning into your body. Feel different parts of your body, establish a connection between your feet and the earth. As you become more adept, extend this practice to your interactions with others. By doing so, you can discern which feelings originate from within you—possibly as a response to the other person's aura or actions—and which feelings belong to your counterpart.

Empathy: Listening and Speaking Without Losing Yourself

Many people mistakenly believe that empathy necessitates fully accommodating the other person, meeting their every wish and need if they are suffering or in distress. This viewpoint often stems from deep-rooted feelings of guilt carried over from childhood. As a child, you may have experienced blame and guilt for the suffering of others, internalizing a belief that their unhappiness was somehow your fault. Children instinctively attribute responsibility to themselves when their parent-child relationship lacks harmony, assuming that something must be wrong with them if their parents are not pleased, reluctant to spend time with them, or unable to find joy in their shared experiences. However, this lingering sense of guilt may feel true but is ultimately unfounded. A child is never to blame if a caregiver is struggling or unhappy.

Similarly, in our present relationships, we are not responsible for our partner's fundamental happiness or their inner struggles. While we bear responsibility for our behavior in the relationship, and to some extent, for contributing to our partner's well-being (which will be discussed further), we cannot shoulder the burden of making them happy or resolving their inner turmoil.

In light of this, many individuals find it easier to create an empathic space for their partner, where they are encouraged to fully express themselves. This ability is essential for fostering intimacy and closeness. Both partners should feel comfortable in the long run: the one who shares and the one who listens and lovingly supports.

Empathy is not:

- Being a mirror that reflects the other person's failings and flawed views: "If only you wouldn't..."
- Constantly inserting one's own opinion: "From my point of view..."
- Minimizing the other person's feelings to make them feel better: "It's not so bad!"

- Feeling responsible for everything: "Now it's my fault again that you don't like this or that about me and that's why you feel bad!"

Empathy means:

- Approaching the other person with openness and goodwill.
- Avoiding immediate self-referencing and instead being genuinely interested in the other person and their experiences.
- Listening to and acknowledging the needs of the other person.
- Allowing the concerns of the other person to exist as they are.
- Being present and actively listening.
- Withholding judgment.

We can cultivate greater empathy by recognizing that we are not responsible for the other person's happiness while still being committed to doing our best.

Many emotionally dependent individuals have a tendency to internalize every negative expression as personal fault or communicate their needs in a way that creates pressure and causes the other person to withdraw. Their longing for someone who cares for them like a parent and tends to their old wounds often leads them to lose touch with themselves and prioritize the other person's reactions over their own experiences.

As a listener...

... they feel criticized and misunderstood.

... they have the impression that only the other person can talk, but they themselves are rarely or never given the opportunity for empathic space.

... they silently scream: "The way you're feeling right now, I feel it all the time too!" They long to be seen and understood themselves.

... they feel obligated to provide the other person with what they themselves need.

... they feel excessively responsible for the other person's well-being, often sacrificing their own perspective to help the other person regain emotional stability.

This kind of empathy is not helpful. Empathy, in its initial stage, is not about taking action. It is about creating a space that allows the other person to simply be.

As an expressor...

... they withhold the real reason for their pain and speak vaguely, fearing they might hurt the other person.

... they are afraid of being too much.

... they closely monitor the other person's reactions instead of fully embracing the empathic space.

... they fear that the space will suddenly be closed, that the other person will become angry, or that they will be rejected.

... they may use the empathic space to transform desires into expectations and reproaches because they have previously suppressed their needs out of fear of being too much or abandoned. The accumulated frustration is then directed toward their partner.

Empathy, therefore, is a value-free and open space that we offer to each other, inviting truthfulness and openness in expression. Initially, how we collectively navigate and respond to each other's expressions and experiences is not the primary focus. This approach creates the best conditions for holding a space and learning to truly open up.

Empathy serves as the healing foundation in relationships. It provides the attention that we may have lacked from our parents in the past. Practicing empathy allows old barriers to gradually dissolve.

Exercises

That way, you can stay connected with yourself when you listen:

- Consciously and deeply breathe in and out, feeling your body.
- Recognize your role in the moment: it is not to save the other person, but to provide an open, receptive, and understanding space for them.
- View the other person's trust as a gift given to you.
- Curiously observe the interplay between the other person's emotions and your own, without judgment. Stay present and attentive. Notice when you tend to mentally disengage and practice staying fully engaged.
- Express gratitude for the other person's openness.

That way, you can stay connected with yourself when you express yourself:

- Make sure that the other person is genuinely open to being there for you.
- Practice expressing what is truly happening by using phrases like "What I actually want to say is...", "Behind this lies...", "I simply wish...", "Ultimately, this is about...".
- Imagine that the space is wide enough to accommodate all aspects of yourself. You are allowed to be fully and authentically present.

> ◆ Maintain a connection with your body. If you find yourself overly focused on the other person's reactions, communicate this: Share your observations about their response, express any fears that arise, and ask for their undivided attention, saying something like, "I sense that you may be disengaging. I'm afraid of overwhelming you. Can you give me your full attention?"

If you find yourself constantly chasing after your partner's attention and only receiving fragmented attention in return, it is important to initiate a discussion. Emotional dependency often arises when one person is giving much more than they are receiving. They may receive some attention and understanding, which gives them hope for improvement, but it never truly fulfills their needs. As a result, they are constantly left waiting and relying on small doses of attention. If you find that your partner is keeping you at a distance and you have been enduring this situation for longer than is beneficial for you, the next chapter on needs becomes particularly important and helpful for you.

Needs

In a relationship based on equality, our needs deserve and must have a place. The question to ask yourself is:

"Who am I in a relationship where every part of me is acknowledged and my needs are valued?"

Emotionally dependent individuals often struggle to take their own needs as seriously as those of their partner. Consequently, the partner tends to do the same, leading to a recurring feeling of being unseen for the dependent person.

If you wish, take a closer look at the needs you have within a relationship. It could be attention, affection, openness, trust, or physical touch, among others.

Write down everything that holds true importance to you. What observations do you make? Can you see if your needs are being acknowledged in the relationship? Do you have the impression that the relationship is meeting these needs? Do you notice a pattern of consistently sacrificing the fulfillment of your needs or repeatedly being with individuals who are unable or unwilling to fulfill these specific needs for various reasons?

Needs are a natural and healthy aspect of being human. Many people mistakenly believe that as they grow older, they should fulfill all their needs independently and that the ultimate goal is complete self-sufficiency. However, this perspective is flawed and can hinder our emotional and spiritual growth. As social beings, we have needs that cannot be met solely by ourselves.

Taking personal responsibility and avoiding emotional dependency involves advocating for these needs, recognizing their importance, and cultivating a social environment in which these needs are acknowledged and respected.

Misunderstandings often arise when discussing neediness. Some view neediness as adopting a victim role due to an inability to assert oneself, while others believe that their well-being is solely the responsibility of their partner and that the relationship exists to fulfill every need.

Neither approach leads to the inner fulfillment we long for. A relationship is not meant to guarantee constant happiness without needs, with the other person perpetually fulfilling everything we require. However, it also doesn't imply constantly separating ourselves and reminding each other of the need for independence.

To achieve emotional autonomy, it is crucial to both assert your needs and learn how to cope when they cannot be met. The first step is committing to future relationships where you can be fully authentic.

Consider which needs align with your true nature when you neither hide nor downplay them. How would you genuinely feel comfortable and seen in a relationship? Which needs should be fulfilled within your romantic partnership, and which can be satisfied through other relationships?

You may discover that you yearn for physical tenderness and emotional affection above all else. Yet, these very needs often get neglected, leaving you dependent on your partner because you've chosen to confine their fulfillment to the relationship. In this context, emotional freedom means clearly communicating your needs and discussing with your partner how these needs can receive the attention they deserve within the relationship.

Valuing your needs, in particular, can gradually dissolve emotional dependency. If you find this challenging, it's worth delving deeper into the underlying reasons. What fears and anxieties arise? How were your needs addressed in the past?

Remember: You are now an adult and no longer reliant on others for survival. You no longer need to conceal your needs in order to endure. You can expect them to be acknowledged—without making your happiness contingent on another person. Importantly, this means you have the agency to exit any situation that does not serve your well-being in the long run. This is a fundamental distinction from the circumstances you experienced as a child.

Inspiration

Describe yourself in writing as the being you perceive yourself to be, including your needs. This exercise brings you closer to understanding your needs and helps you realize that they should not be judged or condemned. Instead, they deserve full presence, as they are not inherently negative but rather a way to experience yourself and others in this world.

Example:

"I am a feeling, sensing, living, perceiving being. I can feel, receive, accept, give away, determine, expect, desire. I can let go, know, and trust. My need is particularly to feel through my skin, to make contact with the world using my body.

> *I crave to be soulfully embraced, recognized, and understood, and to express myself through language. I have a longing to gaze deeply into the eyes of my beloved and experience a profound sense of being at home. I yearn to lie in bed at night with someone who truly knows me, whom I trust deeply, and with whom I feel safe..."*

The best time to discuss your needs with your partner and friends is when you are not currently in conflict. Approach them in a manner that encourages them to embark on a curious journey into your being and character while also expressing how certain things shape and resonate with you. Present yourself as a world waiting to be explored and understood, creating an environment where you can experience how you desire to be treated without the need for hidden messages or assumptions. Similar to how you can find the rules of a new rental apartment in the hallway, you can communicate the rules of living with you to your partner through openly expressed needs. This openness provides your partner with the reassurance of knowing what is expected of them, and it also allows them to openly communicate their thoughts and feelings in return. Communication about needs is a vital aspect of a healthy, mature relationship. It establishes a foundation for seeing each other as individuals who don't wish to inconvenience or exploit one another with their expectations, but rather take good care of themselves and nurture the relationship.

What Am I Truly, and What Behaviors and Habits Can I Adopt?

In a partnership, it is both normal and healthy for us to shift away from our ego-centric way of life and involve our partners in shaping our lives. Compromises are an inherent part of any relationship.

However, these compromises should be made in the right places, where we can accommodate our partner without losing sight of what truly defines us. Take a moment to jot down the aspects of yourself - the behaviors, habits, interests, and needs - that genuinely reflect who you are. Consider how you naturally live when you are single, without aligning yourself with another perso, but rather following your own path.

What are your interests? What character traits distinguish you? How would you describe your personal outlook on life? How have you changed since being in a relationship? Which parts of yourself have you concealed, neglected, or relinquished? Can you identify the moment when you realized, either suddenly or gradually, that you were no longer being true to yourself, compromising your sense of agency?

Understanding the onset of emotional dependence is crucial. It's important to uncover the moments when you started projecting onto your partner what you should have nurtured within yourself.

Example:

Mareike leads a vibrant life as a single woman. She enjoys sailing and parties and values her alone time for creative pursuits. She feels content and attuned to her own needs.

However, once she enters a relationship, Mareike directs a significant amount of attention and energy toward her partner and their connection. In doing so, she tends to neglect her hobbies, lacks sufficient alone time, and focuses primarily on satisfying her partner's needs. Mareike loses herself in the relationship, finding it challenging to remain connected to her own needs and desires. This behavior echoes the role she assumed as a child in caring for her parents. Consequently, being in a relationship for Mareike means sacrificing her own well-being. If her partner feels overwhelmed and withdraws, Mareike experiences a sense of dependence. She has placed her own needs on the back burner and become fully enmeshed with her partner, who now increasingly rejects her. This dynamic leaves Mareike feeling empty, as she receives nothing from her partner and is unable to reciprocate, perpetuating the cycle of connection through sacrifice.

For Mareike, it is crucial to recognize what truly brings her joy and fulfillment and to maintain these habits and behaviors within the relationship. She can learn to establish a new way of relating to her partner that does not rely solely on self-sacrifice. Mareike faces the task of prioritizing self-care and seeking a balanced partnership based on mutual respect. While she may make adjustments to accommodate the relationship, completely abandoning her lifestyle is not advisable.

Here, you will find helpful questions to guide you in staying connected with yourself within a relationship:

- Can I engage in activities that bring me joy simply for the sake of enjoying them? (How can I support others in finding joy if I do not allow myself to experience it?)

Many individuals who experience emotional dependence describe a lack of freedom to experience pleasure and fully indulge in the joys of life without fear. They fear their partner's reactions, constantly consider the impact on the relationship, and overall feel inhibited in their ability to enjoy life. Often, they were shamed for experiencing joy as a child or were deprived of a vibrant and carefree zest for life due to a parent's depression. In a relationship, as soon as they sense similar impulses in their partner, they struggle to maintain their own sense of joy.

It can be beneficial to always remember the activities that bring you joy, even when your partner is not present. Carve out free time and create inner space to integrate fun and happiness into your daily life.

- Where do I hold myself back from fully embracing life, and have I perhaps projected someone onto my partner who dampens my vitality? Does this serve me in perpetuating the old pattern of being hindered?

Emotional dependency can also manifest as difficulty regulating emotions and exerting self-control. Individuals in this situation often allow themselves to be strongly influenced by their partner's emotions and experience significant shifts in their own emotional state within the relationship compared to when they are alone. Often, this pattern operates on an unconscious level: They are accustomed to diminishing the quality of life in partnership because it feels familiar from their childhood. Many individuals internalize beliefs such as "Life isn't enjoyable. Relationships are draining. Relationships require self-sacrifice. Relationships are challenging and filled with sorrow." Consequently, they lose their open-mindedness and zest for life.

◆ How do I prioritize time for myself, take breaks, and allow for moments of solitude?

In order to reconnect with ourselves, it is essential to carve out personal space from time to time. We continually influence and are influenced by others, infecting one another with our emotions. As communicative and social beings, this evolutionary mechanism served as a means of protection from danger and facilitated the rapid transmission of feelings, such as fear in the face of imminent threats, as information from one person to another.

Today, it is important to repeatedly return to our own inner world in order to better engage with ourselves within the context of the larger community. Feeling our own life experiences, engaging in activities without external influence, experiencing a sense of privacy, and expressing ourselves fully provide us with renewed energy and enable us to reflect on what truly matters to us.

This personal connection to our core is our treasure and resource for breaking free from emotional dependency. Along the journey out of this downward spiral, you may suddenly experience an immense sense of relief, a sigh of liberation, and even feelings of happiness from finally reconnecting with yourself, feeling your own emotions, and relying less on external validation. Repeatedly compromising oneself can be endlessly exhausting. However, negative emotions may also surface as you turn your focus inward once again. It is during quiet times and moments of solitude that you can gently and gradually explore your personal concerns and sensitivities. And remember: It feels empowering not to constantly compromise and instead fully embrace and express yourself according to your own desires and preferences.

Chapter 7
Goals and Wishes

*"It's the possibility of having a dream come true
that makes life interesting."*

Paulo Coelho

Emotional dependence acts as a barrier that hinders us from pursuing our own desires and goals. When we solely focus on maintaining our relationship through unhealthy strategies, making ourselves indispensable to our partner, or avoiding abandonment, we deplete our strength and energy. This prevents us from engaging in fulfilling activities, pursuing our interests, and cultivating healthy relationships. As a result, we feel drained, unhappy, and, in severe cases, may even experience mental or physical illness.

Therefore, it is crucial to shift our focus back to our individual desires and goals that exist beyond the confines of our partnership. How much has emotional dependence consumed our thoughts and actions, causing us to lose sight of our values, goals, and dreams? Could there be personal goals and interests that have been neglected or need rekindling? Are we willing to explore abandoned or new directions?

What Holds Us Back?

A sentiment familiar to many individuals struggling with emotional dependence is the belief that they cannot have fun or enjoy life without their partner. "Without you, everything is meaningless" becomes their life motto. They feel the need to do everything together with their partner or, at the very least, require their partner's enthusiasm, approval, and support. Without the affirmation, collaboration, and presence of their partner, fears of growing apart, being abandoned, or creating distance between themselves and their partner arise.

This often manifests in the individual avoiding tasks or activities they suspect their partner may not be enthusiastic about. In doing so, they indirectly assume responsibility for regulating the other person's reactions. Furthermore, they find themselves seeking parental-like validation, similar to a child who constantly seeks reassurance from their parents while exploring new territory. To achieve freedom, one must seek reassurance from within themselves rather than relying on others. When we feel insecure or undecided, it is essential to take a closer look at our desires and intentions. Regardless of external opinions, in the end, we have the autonomy to decide for ourselves. We need to cultivate a sense of competence in our own lives.

Another crucial factor that hinders us from following our own path is the influence of our partner's emotional atmosphere. Naturally, we are attuned to each other's emotions, and our moods can easily be affected by others. We instinctively sense changes in the atmosphere and our own mood when someone enters the room exuding strong emotions—whether it be depression, anger, or radiant joy.

Observe how your outlook on life changes when you are not with your partner. Do you feel more connected to yourself, experience a significant shift, or find yourself interested in completely different things compared to when you are with them? Some individuals become so heavily influenced emotionally that they feel like they have lost touch with their true selves within the relationship. There is no need for shame or feelings of failure in response to this realization—it simply reflects our adaptive nature developed during childhood. However, as adults, we must train ourselves to strengthen our own sense of purpose and fulfillment. If achieving this proves difficult in the presence of our partner, it may be worthwhile to reflect on whether the relationship is truly serving us on our healing journey.

To become free, we require a healing environment. Understanding the extent of external influences on our well-being is crucial. In certain fields, such as professional sports, specialized environment managers work to create the ideal mental and physical setting for athletes to reach their full potential.

Note: It is normal and natural for others to strongly influence us. This should not be seen as a sign of weakness or incompetence. Our responsibility lies in consciously choosing *who* we allow to influence us.

What Brings Me Joy?

Joy serves as a catalyst for our journey toward freedom. When we experience joy in our lives, relationships, and activities, our brain operates at its fullest capacity, and positive hormones flood our system, creating a healthy environment for our body and psyche.

Joy is a desired emotion that most people strive for, but it also renders us vulnerable. Expressing joy opens our hearts and makes us receptive to the positive emotions it evokes. Unfortunately, due to past negative experiences, many individuals shy away from allowing themselves to fully experience joy or even avoid negative emotions, which can impede their ability to fully embrace positive feelings.

True joy cannot be summoned at will, but we can send supportive signals to our body and soul, enabling us to reconnect with joy.

Consider the following practices:

- Physical contact: Choose one or two individuals with whom you feel comfortable receiving frequent and regular physical contact. Whether it's cuddling, receiving a massage, or sharing a warm and loving embrace, these interactions trigger bonding hormones and happiness hormones, which lower stress levels and enhance our receptivity to joy.

- Ritual: Incorporate a small ritual into your daily life that sparks joy for you. It could be savoring a cup of coffee in the morning, spending a day at the pool, engaging in a craft hobby, or any activity that brings you delight. Celebrate the activity and fully immerse yourself in it. Select a ritual that doesn't elicit negative feelings within you. The key is to genuinely feel good about what you are doing. If you find it challenging to engage in something due to a lack of current interest, opt for a peaceful night's rest or reading an inspiring book. Set the bar low. It's not about proving anything to yourself; it's about prioritizing self-care and well-being.

- Reflect on past sources of joy: Make a list of activities or experiences that previously brought you pleasure. What activities did you genuinely enjoy? What triggered positive feelings within you? Which endeavors were driven by intrinsic motivation, and how did that motivation manifest in your body and actions? This exercise is particularly valuable for individuals grappling with emotional dependence as it helps differentiate between activities driven by external factors, such as maintaining a relationship or seeking validation, and those pursued purely out of inner joy. Revisit that point in your life, no matter how long ago it was. You may discover a variation of the activity that aligns better with your present self, but begin from the place where joy was awakened within you.

- Examine how the dynamics of your relationship impact your joy. Identify any old beliefs that resurface and consider whether your partner expresses them directly or indirectly.

  Common examples include:
  ○ What you enjoy doing is not valued by anyone.
  ○ Your pursuits are not deemed interesting enough.

- ○ Other things take precedence; your partner's needs are prioritized.
- ○ Pursuing your personal enjoyment is seen as selfish.
- ○ Your partner believes you are no longer interested in them.
- ○ Your partner feels like they don't recognize you anymore.

Pay attention to instances where your innate sense of joy is stifled by manipulative or unsupportive comments, or where you hold yourself back from engaging in activities you genuinely enjoy. Recognize the long-term implications of these behaviors: envision where you might be in five years if you continue sacrificing joy. Will someone express gratitude for your selflessness? Will your quality of life improve, or will you increasingly feel disconnected from yourself, merely existing rather than truly living? Your current emotions may not immediately align with this conscious thought process, as your inner system is in a vulnerable state. Breaking away from familiar patterns will likely disrupt your attachment system. This is where your mindset becomes crucial, along with your ability to make decisions that prioritize your well-being. This skill can be developed and solidified with the support of friends or therapy.

Remember: Your joy serves as your guide. Allow it to lead you. This is not about seeking temporary substitutes for satisfaction; it's about creating a life that genuinely encompasses joy for you.

My Ideal Relationship(s)

Have you ever wondered about the kind of relationships you truly desire to experience? Perhaps you have always chosen from the limited options presented to you, repeatedly consuming the same dish out of habit. This pattern has inadvertently led you back into emotional dependency, in line with the secret expectations of your inner child. You may be unfamiliar with any other way.

What if you imagined a vast buffet of possibilities for cultivating relationships? If you had complete freedom to shape your relationships, detached from your past experiences, how would you envision them? How would you want the other person to engage with you? Which dormant qualities within yourself would you like to bring to the forefront, waiting to be expressed? How would you prefer to communicate? What kind of shared experiences would you like to have? How would you envision organizing your daily life together? What support and fulfillment would you seek?

In a similar vein, Andrea Lindau states:

"Know who you are and what you want, and invite the other person to join you on the journey. If you stand in your truth and someone else comes closer to you because of it, they belong to you. If they distance themselves just because you take your stand, they are not meant for you."

This concept may seem simple, yet it can also be challenging. However, embracing this mindset is crucial and can transform the dynamics of your relationships, liberating you from emotional dependence.

Inspiration

The easiest way to get in touch with your desires is by becoming aware of how you wish to feel. What emotions do you want to experience in a healthy, fulfilling relationship? What allows you to be both free and securely connected at the same time? What values hold personal significance to you, and which ones do you desire to share with your closest companion?

Your love relationship serves as a space where your emotional well-being and innermost self can flourish. Be bold and discerning in choosing the feelings you want to cultivate, letting go of those that no longer serve you, and recognizing the positive value that the relationship can bring to your life.

Remember: You have the power to determine how love is expressed within your relationship and how it is received and reciprocated. You also have the right to decline gifts and offers.

What Have I Always Wanted to Do?

Do you have a dream? What passion resides within you? What idea is yearning to be nurtured? What goals have you set for yourself? And how have they been suppressed or overlooked due to emotionally dependent relationships?

Emotional dependence often leads us to sacrifice one need for the sake of another. We desire to be true to ourselves, to grow, and to pursue experiences that we have chosen for ourselves. However, we fear that by doing so, we will lose connection with those who are important to us. In our quest for security, even if it is in unhealthy relationships, our dreams, desires, and goals often get neglected. The key is to establish security in a new, healthy way in our lives. As children, we had little control over how security was established. But as adults, we have the power to choose who is truly beneficial for us and where we can find a sense of safety.

A securely attached relationship opens up the realm of possibilities for your dreams and desires. Take the time to write them down. Visualize them. Be fully aware of the joy and fulfillment you will experience when you live life on your own terms.

Inspiration

Make a list of ten small and big wishes that you would like to fulfill within the next three days, three weeks, and three years. Categorize them into short-term and long-term goals. The important thing is to acknowledge and address your desires. Make it a priority to embrace desire and joy again, to make plans, and to feel free.

In our day-to-day lives, breaking free from emotional dependence can often feel challenging. There may be obligations and responsibilities that seem difficult to overcome. However, taking a look at your goals and desires can ignite a spark within you, stimulate your creativity, and give you the courage to explore new paths.

Write down how you will feel when you are fully aligned with yourself and living your life authentically. What kind of person do you aspire to be? How will it feel to inhabit a body you love, engage in activities you are passionate about, and be fully in your element? What does your element look like? How would you recognize yourself and feel recognized? How does the real you move, speak, and make decisions? And most importantly, how can you take steps towards embodying this inner image without overwhelming yourself?

Remember: Your dreams don't always have to be important to others. The most important thing is that they bring you happiness and fulfillment.

Exercises

You can revive your dreams and desires through a series of creative exercises. The following exercises are designed to promote joy and remind you that life can be beautiful.

1. Turn your everyday trip to the supermarket into an experience: Imagine that your dream has already come true, and you are living the free life you desire, whether with or without a partner. Feel fully in your element, free, exuberant, grounded, safe, and happy.

    How do you move? What clothes do you wear? What items do you buy? Which aisles do you visit, and which ones do you skip? Do you have more financial abundance, or do you choose quality over quantity? What shopping decisions does your free self make? You'll be surprised how this idea can influence something as simple as choosing items at the checkout counter.

2. Examine your closet: Your clothes often reflect your self-worth, emotional state, and attitude toward life. Consider how you dress your body: Do you like what you're wearing? Do you feel uncomfortable in certain outfits? Are you wearing clothes that make you look beautiful but feel uncomfortable in your own skin? Why are you doing this and for whom? What kind of clothes would you wear if they positively impacted your well-being and environment? What lifestyle do your clothes reflect? For example, are you predominantly wearing business attire for a job that isn't fulfilling? Are you wearing clothes to please your partner but not yourself? Do you hold onto garments that are old and worn but hold emotional significance? What message do they convey to you?

   Lastly, what type of clothing would you wear if you felt confident, relaxed, and at home in yourself? What makes you feel completely comfortable?

3. Relationships: Reflect on your current relationships. Where is it time to make a change? With whom do you want to deepen your connection and why? What values do you share with others? Where are you trying to impress people you don't genuinely like? Who shows genuine emotional availability and interest in you?

4. Take action towards your dream: Write an email, make a phone call, or send a proposal that brings you one step closer to your dream. Identify the point at which you hold yourself back. What resources do you believe you're lacking, keeping you trapped in inaction? Stepping out of this comfort zone can provide you with a tremendous lift and inspiration. It's important to make a decision: I will pursue this goal. It is my priority. The next step may be challenging but necessary. With my goal in mind, I am willing to take it gladly.

5. Speak your truth: Engage in an open and honest conversation with the person involved and share your inner truth regarding something that is valuable to you. Set boundaries, express your desires, and actively participate in shaping your shared experience. Don't make your wish dependent on the reaction of the other person, but stay true to yourself. This takes immense courage, and you should acknowledge and applaud yourself for taking this action. Observe whether the other person responds positively to your openness and recognizes your needs or if they distance themselves and are unwilling to work towards finding a solution. It may be painful, but prioritizing your authenticity can have a liberating and relieving effect on your emotional well-being.

6. Remove a stress-inducing appointment from your schedule for the next week, which stems from a false sense of responsibility. Replace it with an appointment that brings you joy and is solely for your benefit. This exercise relates to emotional dependence because many

of us lead lives filled with commitments that arise from emotional dependence. For instance, a friendship where the other person constantly unloads their emotional baggage on us, or offers of help that we have made without considering our own energy levels. Take note of how many of these commitments exist in your calendar and how they reflect tendencies towards emotional dependence.

Chapter 8
My Independent Future

"In my perspective, life - including psychotherapy - is exactly about this: becoming a good friend to oneself, getting more choices, and being less fixed on certain reaction patterns."

Dami Charf, "Even Old Wounds Can Heal"

Your future is a culmination of the decisions you make today. This realization may bring about pressure, but it can also be a source of relief. Emotional dependence often accompanies a lingering feeling of powerlessness, where one feels at the mercy of others. The other person holds the reins, and you find yourself following their decisions, daily routines, and mood. However, it can be incredibly liberating to understand and accept that you have the ability to reclaim agency in your own life.

The key is to identify what is holding you back and break free from those attachments. Take the time to explore the main fears that are slowing down your progress:

- The fear of being alone when you take responsibility for designing your life according to your own wishes.
- The fear of being abandoned and not finding someone new.
- The fear of regretting your decisions.
- The fear of feeling guilty and selfish.

- ◆ The fear of failure and losing everything.
- ◆ The fear of finding nothing beyond the horizon despite your hopes.

To confront these fears, it is important to acknowledge them and appreciate your inner protection system for its intention to shield you from pain. Your inner protector is doing its best because you are valuable and important! Now, redirect that need for protection towards healthier avenues. Remember, freeing yourself doesn't mean making reckless decisions. While ending a relationship may be necessary in some cases, it doesn't imply that everything else in your life will crumble into chaos. Try to separate your relationship decisions from the other aspects of your life. What will remain unchanged? What will provide you with a sense of security? Which friends will stand by your side? Will your environment remain the same, or would you consider a move to a place where you feel less alone?

Realize that you will survive. The difficulties and hardships you are currently facing will not persist indefinitely. Choosing yourself will only shake what was not built on a solid foundation to begin with.

In essence, what was not beneficial for you will detach itself. Those things that only provided a false sense of security and failed to satisfy your need for healthy attachment will naturally fade away. Often, emotionally dependent relationships create structures that perpetually induce stress, keeping us trapped in fight-or-flight mode. This constant stress does not protect you or offer true security. At best, it keeps you trapped in a cycle of familiarity.

Make a Decision

Whether you are faced with the decision to end a relationship, make a personal change, set a new course, or bring a long-held dream to fruition, let the decision at hand hold significant importance for you. Set a deadline for yourself to implement the decision.

If the decision feels particularly challenging, it can be helpful to establish a support circle beforehand. Share with trusted individuals what you are going through and ask for concrete steps they can take to support you. Being specific is crucial, as it allows you to step out of dependency and not rely solely on others to instinctively understand your needs. For example, communicate with a friend: "It would mean a lot to me if you could call me every other day for fifteen minutes." Share with your parents: "I would like to stay at your house for a few days because I don't want to be alone right now." Ask another friend: "Could you accompany me to this event on Friday and just enjoy the lightness of life with me? I really need that at the moment." You'll be surprised by how many friends are willing and eager to be there for you. It brings people joy to be able to offer something valuable to others.

Move Forward

After making a decision of great consequence, and even during the process of detaching from emotional dependence, it is important to have a goal to focus on. Embrace the motto of moving on. This means entering a period of reflection, healing, and looking toward the future. You are now ready to take control of your life once again. There may be moments of fear or insecurity that overwhelm you from time to time, and that's normal and okay. During these times, always remember that the moment will pass, and you are not defined by that feeling. You are not the fear that wants to grip you. You are not the longing for the past that held you tightly. You are more than your past patterns. You are not even solely the sum of your past experiences. You encompass your past, your present, and your future. You are your body, your soul, the culmination of your experiences, and the untapped potential that resides within you. Now, it is crucial to bring this potential into the forefront of your attention. You already know what you have experienced, but there is an entire world of new experiences waiting for you to be encountered in a completely different way. The unknown, the new, the feeling of being at home within yourself and experiencing what that truly means may be intimidating, but as you courageously forge ahead into your own future, it will become a healthy and healing habit that feels right, safe, and brimming with joy. By keeping this outlook in mind, a new life attitude that truly aligns with your essence awaits you.

Conclusion

Dear Reader,

By now, you have gained valuable insights into what emotional dependency is, its impact, and how to break free from its grip. As you set this book aside, you may feel a mix of enthusiasm, courage, and some apprehension, wondering, "What's next? How can I apply what I've learned to my everyday life?" With appointments to attend, the return of your partner tonight, and the same routine awaiting you tomorrow, the path forward may seem uncertain.

The art of change lies in patience. The key is to have clarity about where you want to go, while the pace of progress becomes secondary. Be kind and patient with yourself, even if you're not yet ready to make definitive decisions. Remember, achieving emotional independence does not mean relinquishing all relationships and becoming a solitary figure. It means breaking free from the outdated mindset that no longer serves us and consciously reshaping our relationships with a fresh perspective.

Letting go of childish views entails releasing the belief that you are unlovable or to blame. It means recognizing that you have grown beyond the helpless child you once were, no longer at the mercy of others, and no longer bound to desperately prove yourself. Entering a mature, emotionally independent phase in your relationships means acknowledging that any negative self-perceptions stem from past experiences and the conclusions you drew as a child. It involves compassionately processing these experiences and learning to make new choices.

Today, you can embrace the truth that you are a lovable being, deserving of love and recognition. You are not responsible for what happened to you, and you don't have to perpetuate the old drama indefinitely. With each step of self-discovery, your horizons expand, and new paths emerge that lead to different experiences—experiences that align with your true worth.

While it would have been ideal to experience an atmosphere of love and acceptance from the very beginning of your life, you can now confidently declare:

"I am too valuable not to be loved."

With that in mind, have the courage to venture inward and onward. The journey is worthwhile!

Resources and Further Reading

Arterburn, S., & Stoeker, F. (2009). *Every Man's Battle: Winning the War on Sexual Temptation One Victory at a Time*. WaterBrook Press.

Beck, J. S. (2011). *Cognitive therapy: Basics and beyond*. Guilford Press.

Fisher, H. (2004). *Why We Love: The Nature and Chemistry of Romantic Love*. Holt Paperbacks.

Hendrix, H. (2008). *Getting the Love You Want: A Guide for Couples*. St. Martin's Griffin.

Levine, A. (2018). *Attached: The New Science of Adult Attachment and How It Can Help You Find—and Keep—Love*. TarcherPerigee.

Luskin, F. (2002). *Forgive for Good: A Proven Prescription for Health and Happiness*. HarperOne.

Mikulincer, M., & Shaver, P. R. (2007). *Attachment in adulthood: Structure, dynamics, and change*. Guilford Press.

Neff, K. D. (2011). *Self-Compassion: The Proven Power of Being Kind to Yourself*. William Morrow Paperbacks.

Seligman, M. E. P. (2011). *Learned Optimism: How to Change Your Mind and Your Life*. Vintage.

Tatkin, S. (2012). *Wired for Love: How Understanding Your Partner's Brain and Attachment Style Can Help You Defuse Conflict and Build a Secure Relationship*. New Harbinger Publications.

Printed in Great Britain
by Amazon